The
Café Racer
Phenomenon

Those were the days ...

Also from Veloce Publishing –

Those Were The Days ... Series
Alpine Trials & Rallies 1910-1973 (Pfundner)
American 'Independent' Automakers – AMC to Willys 1945 to 1960 (Mort)
American Station Wagons – The Golden Era 1950-1975 (Mort)
American Trucks of the 1950s (Mort)
American Trucks of the 1960s (Mort)
American Woodies 1928-1953 (Mort)
Anglo-American Cars from the 1930s to the 1970s (Mort)
Austerity Motoring (Bobbitt)
Austins, The last real (Peck)
Brighton National Speed Trials (Gardiner)
British Lorries of the 1950s (Bobbitt)
British Lorries of the 1960s (Bobbitt)
British Touring Car Racing (Collins)
British Police Cars (Walker)
British Woodies (Peck)
Café Racer Phenomenon, The (Walker)
Drag Bike Racing in Britain – From the mid '60s to the mid '80s (Lee)
Dune Buggy Phenomenon, The (Hale)
Dune Buggy Phenomenon Volume 2, The (Hale)
Endurance Racing at Silverstone in the 1970s & 1980s (Parker)
Hot Rod & Stock Car Racing in Britain in the 1980s (Neil)
Last Real Austins 1946-1959, The (Peck)
MG's Abingdon Factory (Moylan)
Motor Racing at Brands Hatch in the Seventies (Parker)
Motor Racing at Brands Hatch in the Eighties (Parker)
Motor Racing at Crystal Palace (Collins)
Motor Racing at Goodwood in the Sixties (Gardiner)
Motor Racing at Nassau in the 1950s & 1960s (O'Neil)
Motor Racing at Oulton Park in the 1960s (McFadyen)
Motor Racing at Oulton Park in the 1970s (McFadyen)
Superprix – The Story of Birmingham Motor Race (Page & Collins)
Three Wheelers (Bobbitt)

Enthusiast's Restoration Manual Series
Yamaha FS1-E, How to Restore (Watts)

Essential Buyer's Guide Series
BMW GS (Henshaw)
BSA Bantam (Henshaw)
BSA 500 & 650 Twins (Henshaw)
Harley-Davidson Big Twins (Henshaw)
Hinckley Triumph triples & fours 750, 900, 955, 1000, 1050, 1200 – 1991-2009 (Henshaw)
Honda CBR600 (Henshaw)
Honda FireBlade (Henshaw)
Honda SOHC fours 1969-1984 (Henshaw)
Norton Commando (Henshaw)
Triumph Bonneville (Henshaw)
Vespa Scooters – Classic 2-stroke models 1960-2008 (Paxton)

General
BMW Boxer Twins 1970-1995 Bible, The (Falloon)
British 250cc Racing Motorcycles (Pereira)
BSA Bantam Bible, The (Henshaw)
Ducati 750 Bible, The (Falloon)
Ducati 750 SS 'round-case' 1974, The Book of the (Falloon)
Ducati 860, 900 and Mille Bible, The (Falloon)
Edward Turner: The Man Behind the Motorcycles (Clew)
Funky Mopeds (Skelton)
Kawasaki Triples Bible, The (Walker)
Lambretta Bible, The (Davies)
Laverda Twins & Triples Bible 1968-1986 (Falloon)
Moto Guzzi Sport & Le Mans Bible, The (Falloon)
Motorcycle Apprentice (Cakebread)
Motorcycle Road & Racing Chassis Designs (Noakes)
Off-Road Giants! – Heroes of 1960s Motorcycle Sport (Westlake)
Redman, Jim – 6 Times World Motorcycle Champion: The Autobiography (Redman)
Scooter Lifestyle (Grainger)
Triumph Bonneville!, Save the – The inside story of the Meriden Workers' Co-op (Rosamond)
Triumph Motorcycles & the Meriden Factory (Hancox)
Triumph Speed Twin & Thunderbird Bible (Woolridge)
Triumph Tiger Cub Bible (Estall)
Triumph Trophy Bible (Woolridge)

Velocette Motorcycles – MSS to Thruxton New Third Edition (Burris)

From Veloce Publishing's new imprints:

Battle Cry!
Soviet General & field rank officer uniforms: 1955 to 1991 (Streather)
Red & Soviet military & paramilitary services: female uniforms 1941-1991 (Streather)

Hubble & Hattie
Clever Dog! (O'Meara)
Complete Dog Massage Manual, The – Gentle Dog Care (Robertson)
Dinner with Rover (Paton-Ayre)
Dog Cookies (Schops)
Dog Games – Stimulating play to entertain your dog and you (Blenski)
Dogs on wheels (Mort)
Dog Relax – Relaxed dogs, relaxed owners (Pilguj)
Excercising your puppy: a gentle & natural approach (Robertson)
Know Your Dog – The guide to a beautiful relationship (Birmelin)
Living with an Older Dog (Alderton & Hall)
My dog has cruciate ligament injury (Häusler)
My dog has hip dysplasia (Häusler)
My dog is blind – but lives life to the full! (Horsky)
My dog is deaf (Willms)
Smellorama – nose games for dogs (Theby)
Swim to Recovery: Canine hydrotherapy healing (Wong)
Waggy Tails & Wheelchairs (Epp)
Walkin' the dog – motorway walks for drivers and dogs (Rees)
Winston ... the dog who changed my life (Klute)
You and Your Border Terrier – The Essential Guide (Alderton)
You and Your Cockapoo – The Essential Guide (Alderton)
You and Your Cockapoo – The Essential Guide (Alderton)

www.veloce.co.uk

First published in September 2009. Reprinted December 2010 by Veloce Publishing Limited, Veloce House, Parkway Farm Business Park, Middle Farm Way, Dorchester, Dorset, DT1 3AR. Fax 01305 268864/e-mail info@veloce.co.uk/web www.veloce.co.uk or www.velocebooks.com.
ISBN: 978-1-845842-64-2 UPC: 6-36847-04264-6

Readers with ideas for automotive books, or books on other transport or related hobby subjects, are invited to write to the editorial director of Veloce Publishing at the above address.
British Library Cataloguing in Publication Data – A catalogue record for this book is available from the British Library. Typesetting, design and page make-up all by Veloce Publishing Ltd on Apple Mac. Printed in India by Replika Press.

Contents

Introduction

It is impossible to capture 50 years of motorcycling history in one book, even one strand of it such as the café racer phenomenon. This book is a taster, a general history which I hope will spark a deeper interest within anyone who rides a motorcycle.

The reason that so many riders modify their machines is to stand out from the pack. To own something different, a motorbike that has a little extra, somehow makes it more personal, an extension of why you ride. That ethos has not changed in half a century, and never will, so long as there are motorcycles.

This book partly traces the mechanical development of the café racer, the quest for more speed, sweeter handling and better brakes – but this book isn't just about technical improvements or a list of race winners.

This is also a social history of Britain – especially working-class Britain – from the '50s, when almost the whole country, except for cafés, closed at 5pm sharp, to the late 20th century revival in café racer culture. It contains personal memories from dozens of riders, from the '50s to the present day. My father's generation, for example, discovered rock 'n' roll, Elvis, and rode fast bikes and on roads without speed limits. It also saw some 7000 people die on Britain's roads each year.

The Rockers of the '60s gave the tabloid press of the time a reason to denigrate anyone on two wheels, but the prosaic truth is that most riders in that decade simply wanted a decent bike, and perhaps occasionally to race their mates.

The '70s saw older riders tempted by the superbikes from Japan, Britain and Italy, with their sheer power, sporty styling and sometimes dubious handling.

An alternative motorcycle industry in Britain helped solve those chassis problems, and accessorised a café racer lifestyle, yet that industry all but vanished in the '80s.

The urge to tweak a motorcycle, however, is like an itch that begs to be scratched. The bikers of the modern era are just as keen as their predecessors on tuning engines, modifying the chassis or adding a few personal touches. The spirit of the café racer is all about having fun, a place to meet, and showing off your own version of motorcycle cool.

Long may it continue.

Acknowledgements

The author would like to thank the following people, who helped make the book possible by providing contact numbers, memories, chasing up photographs, and capturing the essence of the café racer scene in different decades.

Brian at the Busy Bee Club, Bob Brooks, Dave Bryan, Steve Carpenter, Mike Cook, Pete Coombs, Paul Cooper, Dave 'Crasher' Croxford, Mitch Curran, Anthony Curzon, Gip Dammone, Paul Dunstall, Kate Emery, John Hartas, Del Hooper, Father Graham Hullett, Norman Hyde, Val at Gus Kuhn, Eamon Maloney, Will Mellor, Steve Murray, Steve at Nirvana Motorcycles, Len Patterson, Malcolm Powell, Ralph and Eve Pilkington, Lawrence Rose, Dan Sagar, Harry Scarsbrook, Pete Schneider, Jeff Stone, Graham Tansley, Jackie at Unity Equipe, Mark Wilsmore, Harry Winch, Ed Wright.

This book is dedicated to the lovely Anne.

Foreword by Paul Dunstall

It's hard to imagine now, but motorcycling in Britain was very different back in the 1950s. Open roads, no speed limits and a wide variety of motorcyles available for a young rider to choose from.

But once you had the bike, where did you go? To the local café of course, where your skill and your machine's performance could be – legally – put to the test. Thinking about those days brings back some great memories ...

With a Vincent Rapide in my sights, I'm away from Johnson's Café, onto the A20 and flat on the tank, using maximum revs up through the gears along the deserted A2. I'm passing Brands Hatch circuit, the Dominator's speedo showing 120mph round the long, left-hand curve, leading onto what is now called Death Hill.

Then watching the speedo needle slowly creep to 125mph down the hill, holding it flat out until the braking point, down into third for the left hand curve at Knats Valley. Back on the throttle and over the Farningham crossroads at 90mph, carrying that speed up the long drag to Swanley ... then sitting up and easing off the speed as I approach the Burmac Café. Checking behind to see where the Vincent rider is, wave or nod in acknowledgement at a terrific 'dice'.

After dark we would travel further along the A20 to the 'mad mile', to race flat out from the traffic lights at Mottingham, then down to the Dutch House pub café. Thinking back,

I realise that the term 'café racer' hadn't even been invented then, but it is a perfect description of what was going on. Young guys having fun and meeting up at the few places where leather jackets, noisy motorbikes and quiffs were welcome in '50s Britain.

I was just 17 when I started doing all this on a brand new 600cc Norton Dominator, and I soon started experimenting with ideas to increase its performance. Simple changes like setting the sit-up-and-beg handlebars in the downwards position and fitting a 'droop snoot' mini fairing. That added a good 5mph. With many more tweaks, my Dominator soon evolved into a very competitive machine. Practice days at Brands Hatch beckoned, where I quickly discovered the need for

Paul Dunstall at a track test in the '60s.

5

more cornering clearance and more performance. Modifications were made on a weekly basis, and were tested every Wednesday at Brands.

I raced the Domi for a season before handing it over to Fred Neville, and our successes (by then the bike was visibly quicker than a good Manx Norton) generated a great deal of interest from other Norton Dominator owners. Many of them visited my workshop, located at the back of my father's scooter shop, and it was there that the Dunstall Café Racer business started.

I kept spare sets of upswept exhaust pipes hanging on the workshop wall, ready to replace any damaged by a fall on track. Norton owners began pestering me for a pair, and five spare sets soon went, then twenty sets quickly disappeared. So, just out of enthusiasm for improving the road bikes of the day, the Paul Dunstall Café Racer business had begun.

As café racer popularity took off in the '60s,

demand for Dunstall bikes and equipment became worldwide. I ended up making bikes for famous faces of the era, including Steve McQueen, then importers like Yamaha Europe, Kawasaki, Suzuki GB, Norton Villiers Group and more. I also made many friends in the world of motorcycling, where the competition was generally good-natured and some great characters raced for the fun of it, more than anything else.

Although I am no longer active in the motorcycle industry, I marvel at the astonishing performance and handling of today's sportsbikes. The bikes have changed beyond anything we could have imagined back in the '50s, and although most of the cafés have long gone, I hope this book brings back happy memories for older riders, and gives younger bikers a glimpse of a more carefree time.

Safe riding,

Paul Dunstall

The Rockers ride

Like rock 'n' roll, the café racer is an integral part of the '50s, with its roots in the previous decades.

The '50s motorcycle riders who dressed like Gene Vincent, modified their own motorbikes, and raced each other along the A-roads of Britain, weren't doing anything very different from the young men who rode motorcycles in the '20s, '30s or '40s. The same spirit of adventure links Lawrence of Arabia's motorcycling exploits in the '20s to the jukebox racers of the '50s. It's about testing the machine, and yourself, to the limits.

There were fast bikes in the '30s and '40s, like the Vincent, Brough-Superior twins, Ariel Square Four, or the first factory 'race replicas' such as the Velocette KTT and BSA's Gold Star 350/500cc singles, but these were often bought by wealthy motorcycle enthusiasts. Before the '50s, very few younger riders could afford a decent 250cc motorbike, never mind a large capacity machine. Many fast models, like the first Norton Dominators of the '50s, were for export only – British riders couldn't buy them, even if they had the money.

It took a unique set of social, economic, and cultural factors to bring about that very British creation, the café racer.

As the '50s progressed, there was an increasing domestic supply of British motorcycles, plus easier access to hire purchase credit (essentially borrowing money and repaying it weekly). In 1950, petrol came off ration, along with soap, and then the rationing of many staple foodstuffs ended in 1954.

Life seemed to be slowly improving, and the younger generation – which could barely recall the misery of wartime Britain – wanted some fun. Cafés were in every

A regular at the Skyways café, Howard Hunt is pictured here with his BSA Gold Star 500. This sporting single was in production from the '30s to the '60s. In the background is a Manx Norton that was raced by Rex Watchorn; also a Skyways regular from Manchester. (Courtesy Howard Hunt)

The Busy Bee was located on the A41, which was an arterial route north before the M1 motorway was constructed. (Courtesy Busy Bee Club)

town and city, and dotted along the arterial roads of Britain. Many had sections where 'youths' were actually welcome, even on motorbikes!

Places like the Ace Café and Busy Bee had opened their doors in the '30s, and back then were known as 'pull-ins'. All kinds of delivery drivers, commercial travellers and Sunday drivers used these cafés, as Britain had no motorways until 1958.

Triton-builder Dave Degens recalled that as a child in the '40s, he would visit the Ace Café with his father:

"Dad would drop in the transport café section during the week, but on Sundays, with a collar and tie on, he would take us to the posh half of the Ace, which was a fully kitted-out restaurant. We might have a legendary knickerbocker glory ice cream there – magic."

Many cafés had a so-called youths' section, which was separate from the transport café or tourist-orientated half of the business. This area would often have a jukebox, table football maybe, plus an espresso coffee machine from Italy. Some cafés, like the Ace and the Busy Bee at Watford, were open 24 hours a day, a novelty in an era when most of Britain closed shop at 5pm, on the dot.

It doesn't sound much, but in mid-1950s austerity Britain, teenage lads suddenly found they had a place where they were welcome, parents were rarely seen, and girls regularly showed up.

The Café Continental was on the main Manchester Road in Oldham, and riders would gather to speed test their machines from the '40s onwards, or meet up before going to watch a trials event on the moors nearby.
The picture is believed to have been taken in the '50s, and shows a pair of 350cc Velocette Vipers. A group of men, probably trials riders or keen spectators judging by their sturdy clothing, watch the action. Note that only one rider appears to own a crash helmet, which was typical of an era when flat caps, or no headgear at all, was the norm. (Courtesy Harry Scarsbrook)

The Unicorn Café in Leeds, also known as Salvo's Transport Café for a while. Pictured are Salvo and his family who lived on the premises, and occasionally allowed gambling in the back room. (Courtesy Gip Dammone)

Howard Hunt looking sharp on his 500 Goldie in the '60s. Note the cut-down front mudguard, the clip-on handlebars set onto the fork legs, and Howard's winkle-picker shoes, drainpipe jeans and quiff.

Northern brewed

This café scene was nationwide, from the Busy Bee at Watford, the Clock Tower in Exeter, and Johnson's on the A20 near Brands Hatch, to the Unicorn in Leeds, the Continental in Oldham, and Skyways in South Manchester.

Harry Scarsbrook recalled his uncle visiting the Café Continental regularly in the late '40s and during the '50s.

"My uncle, Eddie Bardsley, was a keen trials man. He also owned a motorbike repair shop on King Street, Oldham. Eddie was keen on photography and liked to record some of the moorland trials events. He also photographed the trials riders relaxing at the Continental.

"I was only 15 when I started going to Skyways. In the '60s Sunday nights were the night to be there, and Derek and Pauline Harrison, the owners, opened a club downstairs in the cellar, which was accessed through a trap door in the middle of the floor of the coffee bar. Health and Safety would have had a field day if it had been in existence then!

Squires café at Sherburn-in-Elmet, near Leeds, was one of the biggest crowd-pullers in the '60s.
(Courtesy The Mike Cook Collection)

"I recall an unlucky September 13th, it was back in 1965, and that evening, leaving the Skyways at some crazy speed, I crashed into the side of a VW Beetle, about 100 yards along Styal Road. I suffered minor injuries, but my girlfriend, (whose parents forbade her to ride on the back of my bike) suffered a fractured skull, because she didn't have a helmet on, which at that time weren't compulsory. Luckily we lived to tell the tale."

Coffee bar cowboys

Hardly any high-performance British bikes back then were aimed at young people, but youngsters aspired to own and tune them.

"Most bikes then were boring, everyday transport," remembers Ed Wright, who was an apprentice at the BSA factory in 1957. "We all wanted something faster, with brakes, lights and tyres that worked."

Another BSA worker at that time was Dave Bryan, who started off on a 250, then moved to a Gold Star 350.

"I had all the kit on that Goldie, and I thought – like many young lads then – that I was immortal. We raced to Tamworth Station Café and people would park along the main straight to spectate. We took off over the hump-back bridge on the straight. We formed our own club, the Moorfield Eagles, with a big eagle painted onto the back of our jackets. Cool eh?"

Times were different before the introduction of the national speed limit in the UK.

"One thing I recall was the flexible attitude of the police. Often I just got a stern telling off. One copper made me walk home, pushing my bike, after he pulled me for speeding in town. That was my punishment, being escorted home by the law to face my parents."

The roots of the Triton

Modifying your bike, or building a special, was commonplace in the '50s and '60s, and that was how the Tribsa, Norvin and Triton, plus many more combinations of engines and frames, all came about.

The most famous amalgamation of two brands, the Triton, was the logical result of a decade of intense competition by two market-leading motorcycle companies, Triumph and Norton. Both were rivals on the track and in the showroom, with unique strengths and weaknesses.

Norton was a brand renowned for good handling. The Featherbed chassis, developed by Rex and Cromie McCandless in the late 1940s, was acknowledged as the racer's choice, the best-handling framework that a fast British bike could have at that time.

Rex McCandless had worked in the aviation industry during WWII, and thought it ridiculous that motorcycles

Harry Winch takes his café racer for a spin back in the early '70s.

Harry Howarth put a BSA A10 twin-cylinder engine sideways in a Sunbeam frame, thus creating a 'Beesun.' He then added a sporting sidecar.

Triton engine detail.

used a crude, badly sprung, Victorian bicycle chassis. So McCandless designed a swinging arm suspension system, which he called a 'Spring Heel', and fitted it to a bicycle, then to a grass track race machine. BSA tried it on a scrambler and it won easily. The Spring Heel worked far better than a rigid rear end.

The restless McCandless took his ideas to Norton in the late '40s. It paid him to set up a design office in Northern Ireland and create a racing frame for its Manx 350/500 singles. Using twin downtubes, with extra bracing around the headstock, and entirely made from Reynolds 531 tubing, the Featherbed frame instantly became renowned as the best available. The Norton Featherbed's first race was in 1950, and riders started winning immediately.

Meanwhile, Triumph was equally renowned for the speed of its twin-cylinder engines. Turner had designed the Speed Twin 500 back in the 1930s, and after WWII, he set about refining his concept, tweaking every last gasp of power from the pre-unit twins, making them bigger and faster.

Triumph proved its bikes were rapid at the TT races, or by entering continental speed trials and endurance races. Most famously in the late '50s, at Bonneville Salt Flats in Utah, Johnnie Allen set a land speed record on the 650 Tiger, thus inspiring the Bonneville 650 model for the 1959 sales year.

So the Triton was the perfect partnership, a logical blend of ton-up speed and secure handling.

The final piece of the jigsaw was the introduction of a low-budget car racing formula in the early 1950s. The rules were that drivers could make their own small race car, but use an engine no bigger than 500cc. Norton wouldn't sell engines, only complete bikes, to these aspiring racing drivers, so a steady supply of unwanted

A Dresda Triton; note details like the engine plates, central oil tank and exposed fork springs. Dave Degens established his Dresda Triton's credentials in 1965 by winning the Barcelona 24-hour race on it.

Featherbed frames began to appear throughout the '50s and early '60s.

The scene was set for a generation of British riders to discover the joy of building their own race-inspired specials. The era of the café racer had dawned.

Degens always recommended setting the Triumph engine upright, not canted forward, to prevent oil feed problems.

Ed Wright and some of the Tamworth Station Café crowd check out a race machine at an early '60s road race meeting. (Courtesy Ed Wright)

Dave Croxford in action, sidecar racing in the late '50s.

Make do and mend

Many young motorcyclists might have aspired to owning a café racer, but they often made do with something more humble, or made some modifications to what they had.

"Because I worked at BSA Small Heath I wanted a Gold Star, but couldn't afford it on apprentice wages. So I decided to make the best B33 I could." recalled Ed Wright. "The great thing was that as an employee you could get free parts from the factory, so I fitted a gas-flowed head, special carb, lighter valve gear, new front brake, etc. It had Ace 'bars fitted and I suppose it was my own version of a Goldie – just cheaper."

This culture of pilfering was fairly typical of the era in British manufacturing. Road racer Dave Croxford was a young toolmaker back in the '50s and often used 'spare' bits of aluminium dural or steel to fabricate parts which he sold to his mates. It was common for many riders to make their own modifications, as very few aftermarket suppliers were around in the late '50s.

"You had to literally draw something out on cardboard, then cut it out as a pattern, before making in metal," commented Dave Croxford, who started his biking career at the Ace Café, before taking to the track as a sidecar racer, then solo competitor in the '60s and '70s.

"Nobody really knew anything, I mean if you set the points using a light to find top dead centre, well, that was considered expert tuning. If you wanted rear sets, you got someone like me to make them, same with engine plates, fuel tanks ... you couldn't go to a bike shop and buy all this stuff."

Dave modified his own machines and liked to visit the Ace Café to see what people were doing with their bikes.

"I owned a BSA Gold Star on HP as a teenager. But I lost my licence, bit of a stitch-up with the law really, but the upshot was I couldn't make the payments on the Goldie, and the bike was re-possessed. So while I was banned I built a Manx Norton café racer, using the engine and Featherbed frame from my sidecar race outfit.

"It was a quick bike and I used to wear racing leathers, show off a bit, taking the Neasden bridge bend pretty fast. I thought I was the bee's knees, and I suppose building the Manx café racer helped me flog a few bits to lads at the Ace. Then I crashed the bike into a concrete barrier and decided I'd go road racing as I thought it was safer. Little did I know I was going to have over 270 crashes on track!

Dave 'Crasher' Croxford is still in one piece today, and famously never broke a major bone in his body in all those crashes. Many famous racers of the '60s began their careers by hanging around cafés and tweaking their machines to prove themselves among the fast lads.

Harry Winch recalled some street racing at Johnson's Café on the A20.

"Johnson's was set on a hill and there was a fairly long straight nearby. The lads used to get flat on the tank to see who had the fastest bike. I think at one stage the café owners had a kind of trophy or prize system going to encourage it. On a good day some 200 bikes would gather at Johnson's. Bill Ivy started racing there."

Dave Croxford with a summons from the '60s. He's a reformed character nowadays.

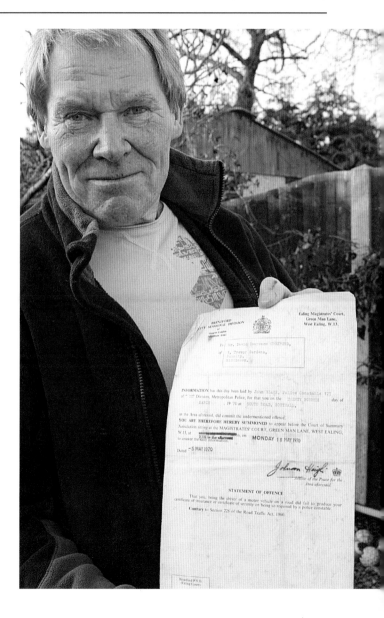

visit any
WETHERED
pub

and enjoy that
Strong Country
Flavour

In the late '60s, Café Jak was one of the main hangouts in Maidenhead. (Courtesy The Mike Cook Collection)

The mythical wild ones

The popular mythology is that hundreds of rebellious young men suffered serious injury or death by taking part in so-called 'suicide runs' or racing through city traffic whilst records were spinning on the jukebox. If you ask those who were there, the story is a little more mundane than the tabloid hysteria of the time.

"I went to Johnsons regularly between 1960-69," remembered Harry Winch, "and I never saw the suicide run, or heard of it taking place. The idea that two of you would ride straight at each other, at 100mph, and see who would swerve at the last second just seemed daft to us."

Harry saw some racing, but very little trouble during his decade hanging out at Johnsons.

"The papers were full of Mods vs Rockers stories in the mid-'60s, but my impression is that half the time journalists simply made it up. Myself and my mates were once offered £5 each if we started a fight with some Mods one Sunday – we just laughed."

Meanwhile Dave Croxford recalled how generally sedate the scene was at the Ace Café in London.

"Generally it was quiet at the Ace – the tales of people lining the banking and egging on lads doing the ton past the café every week are rubbish. I know, I was there in the '50s. As regards fights, I never saw anything violent in those days."

But the popular mythology of the day was that these 'wild' youths were trouble-makers. An episode of *Dixon of Dock Green* – a top-rated police drama of the '60s – showed 'ton-up' boys as speed-obsessed law-breakers, hell-bent on risking every road user's life. Then on 9th February 1961, the *Daily Mirror*, the biggest selling daily newspaper in the UK, screamed "Suicide club – it devours 130,000 members every year!" from its front page.

The paper focussed on the Ace Café in particular, and featured some of the regular visitors. Mark Wilsmore, who runs the Ace Café today, takes up the story:

"A few lads saw the TV show, the 'suicide club' story, and basically jeered a few local cops, maybe threw some tea at their van as they went past the Ace. The police at Harlesden then over-reacted. There was no planned 'raid' as such, local cops got the hump and came down mob-handed. It was a little thing that got out of control."

Troublemakers existed, but as Ed Wright recalled not everyone wanted to be associated with 'coffee bar racers', or Rockers as they came to be labelled after the Margate and Brighton clashes with Mods later in the '60s.

"Some fast riders didn't want to be known as Rockers, so they wouldn't wear the gear, or ride something with Ace 'bars, single seat and all that. I recall racing one guy to Tamworth and he had a Velocette 500 with straight handlebars, dual seat and massive canvas panniers on it, yet the bike was really rapid. Fast rider, just not a ton-up boy."

Bob Brooks was a regular at both the Ace Café and the Busy Bee in the late '50s and early '60s, but never considered himself part of the café racer scene.

"I had a Triumph Tiger 110," said Bob, "and joined the Triumph Owners' Club as I liked the social side of things. I was a slower rider, didn't race people, but that never bothered me, I was happy. The only modifications I have made in 50 years of ownership are fitting a Siamese 2-into-1 exhaust and a touring fairing."

Pete Coombs remembered going to Brands Hatch back in '61 with his mate Ian, who had a café-style Francis Barnett 225cc machine.

Pete Coombs and his mate would visit Brands Hatch in the '60s, sometimes two-up on a Francis Barnet; other times Pete would ride a 65cc Dunkley.

"It had all the kit on; megaphone exhaust, clip-ons, rear sets, single seat. We once got an indicated 70mph from it – in third! Sadly, the bike actually slowed down when Ian put it in top gear."

Jeff Stone and his immaculate-looking Triton, taken in 1967.

Jeff Stone, who is now Press Officer for the BMF riders' rights group in the UK, sums up the scene for many UK riders in the '60s;

"I saved money, built myself a nice T120 Triton, and just enjoyed riding around with my mates on it. Didn't go looking for trouble, just some fun. Like many guys back then, I had to sell the bike to raise a deposit on a house. But the café racer I had was part of my youth, part of growing up, they were great days."

Putting on the style

What began as a hobby for everyday riders soon became a fledgling café racer industry, as tuners, parts and accessory manufacturers all realised there was money in the phenomenon.

When Dave Degens established Dresda Autos in the early '60s, to build and refine his own Triton concept, Eddie Dow, Paul Dunstall and Geoff Dodkin were already making a selection of performance parts for various Brit bikes, or creating their own modified machines, often for clubman road racing.

BSA dealer Eddie Dow was an ex-BSA Gold Star racer, and in the '50s began to offer a range of tuning and chassis parts for the Goldies. Eddie Dow top yokes and uprated brakes were considered almost essential for any 'kitted-up' BSA twin or single. Other dealers, like Deeprose and Geoff Dodkin who specialised in Velocette, or Reg Dearden, Gander & Gray, Bill Chuck and more, all put time and effort into improving the motorcycles they sold.

This neat ruse of getting someone else to do the development work was typical of the British motorcycle industry during the '50s and '60s, when it was drifting into decline despite selling thousands of machines every week. Just as a new wave of Japanese motorbikes began to appear, total complacency at managerial level, and a lack of long term investment were hastening the end of the British bike industry.

"My boss at Triumph, Doug Hele, could take almost any bike off the production line and make it a Daytona winner," recalled Triumph tuner Norman Hyde, who worked at Meriden. "But the management structure at Triumph in the '60s wasn't interested in

Dealers like Deeprose and Dodkins helped develop the Velocette Venom as a credible clubman racer.

making everyday bikes faster, better handling or applying advanced technology. It was both immensely interesting and endlessly frustrating being in the Triumph race development shop."

Norman Hyde wheelies his T150 drag racer off the line.

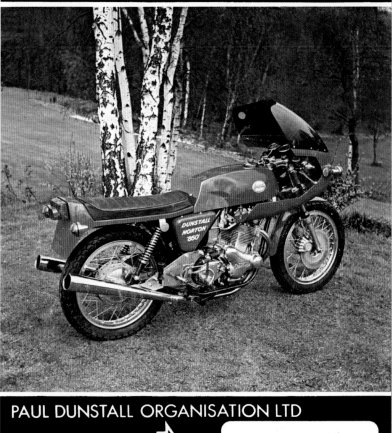

dunstall equipment

PAUL DUNSTALL ORGANISATION LTD

DUNSTALL EQUIPMENT STOCKIST ➡

Paul Dunstall's tuning tips were part of his early catalogues in the '60s. Paul Dunstall expanded his range of Norton goodies throughout the '60s and '70s, and this '70s Commando is a fully 'Dunstallized' Norton twin.

Ed Wright felt the same frustration at BSA during the '60s.

"BSA knew how to make fast bikes, better handling machines and accessorise them. But there was no willpower from the top. Testing was almost a joke sometimes, I often tested new bikes wearing office suits and shoes for example, and once crashed a scooter then fixed it up when my boss wasn't about.

"I remember one day they bought a Suzuki Super Six 250 to take it apart, see how it was made. I knew then, that we were in trouble – whatever we did with a BSA C15 250 it would never compete with the Suzuki."

But this lack of investment in model development by the big factories left the door wide open for almost anyone, from a keen amateur engineer in his shed to a large motorcycle retailer, to start manufacturing engine tuning goodies, suspension tweaks, better brakes, etc.

"I had upswept exhausts made for my Dominator in the late '50s," recalled Paul Dunstall, "and the demand just mushroomed. Ace 'bars, single seats, rear sets, then tuning kits for the Norton and Triumph twins. Within a few years I'd gone from selling scooters to South London commuters to running a worldwide mail order business. It was incredible."

By the mid-'60s the café racer boom was in full swing. Even staid manufacturer Velocette had tweaked its Venom, producing a clubman version, whilst

The Rickman chassis started as a framework for tough, 500cc off-road racing, and strong headstock bracing was a fundamental part of the design

A BSA Rocket III at the M1 services near London in the early '70s (Courtesy Vic Bing)

Royal Enfield went further and made the cute little Continental GT250 – arguably the only true factory café racer made by the British industry. Triumph made the Bonneville Thruxton in 1965, to celebrate its success in the Thruxton 500 Mile road race.

But although the factories dabbled, the independent tuners and chassis specialists were the ones making advances in performance, handling and braking – and then selling it to the public.

Brothers Don and Derek Rickman were keen to try the new café racer market for their off-road Metisse chassis, which they had developed whilst motocross racing in the late '50s. In 1966, Rickman launched a café racer rolling chassis capable of taking Triumph 500/650 twins.

Made from Reynolds 531 tubing, just like the Featherbed frame, the Rickman tubework was bronze-welded and nickel-plated, giving it a polished look. The bracing around the headstock was substantial, as you might expect on a off-roader, which made the frame appealing to competition riders.

Rickman had already tried asking the big manufacturers for engines, so it could make complete bikes, but it was turned down. The same response came back when it offered its frame-making services to AMC and the Triumph-BSA group. But although BSA officially refused to work with Rickman, it wasn't too proud to pinch a few ideas.

"I was working in the BSA design department in the mid-'60s," recalled Ed Wright, "and we had the BSA-Triumph triple-cylinder bikes being developed from about '63 onwards. The back end of the BSA Rocket III, launched in '68, was basically a copy of the Rickman Metisse frame. It worked, so BSA copied it."

Paul Dunstall found that despite producing quick Norton racers in the '60s, he was never considered a potential house specialist in tuning until it was too late.

"Norton's Bracebridge Street race shop always saw us as competition, tried to keep things secret from us," commented Paul. "It was only as they were going bust in the early '70s that they approached me and offered to sell me some racing parts, prototype bikes, etc."

Dave Croxford was the first racer to win using a disc brake, at Mallory in the mid-'60s.

"Colin Lyster designed the disc brake, he made it from cast iron, with the carrier and everything. He had approached the big British companies but they weren't interested, so I rode my Gus Kuhn Norton with one. People laughed, but I won with it. Then Lockheed took it over, bought Colin's patents, and eventually it found its way onto bikes – but Honda were the first to use it on a mass market machine, not Norton, Triumph or BSA."

With hindsight, perhaps it's a harsh judgement to blame the British motorcycle factories too much for their lack of progress. The '60s was the decade of the car boom in Britain, the USA and much of Europe. Motorcycle sales were in decline, and the '50s Rockers were getting married, trading in their Tritons for Ford Cortinas or Austin Minis.

"I built a café racer in my council flat"

Irrespective of what was happening in the motorcycle industry, the café scene evolved from the grass roots and thrived in the '60s.

The desire to be different and create a machine that would stand out in a crowd – whether at the Unicorn in Leeds, the Old Manor in Berkshire, or the Dug-out in Golders Green – remained buoyant in the '60s, even as mainstream motorcycle sales took a nosedive in Britain.

Eric Patterson at Beaulieu in 2004, aboard a JAP-engined Norton café racer. Eric set a land speed record at Bonneville on this bike in 2008.

Eric Patterson on his BSA Super Rocket (right) and his mate, Eddie Bartlett. Eric saved money back then by sometimes cutting his own hair, hence the pointy quiff.

"I had a BSA Super Rocket in the '60s," recalled Eric Patterson, "and I used to test any improvements I'd made along the four-mile straight on the way to the Old Manor Café. That was a posh place, located in a big country house."

Anthony Curzon's Norton café racer, built in his London council flat.

Anthony Curzon was dreaming of better things whilst owning an Enfield Crusader Sports.

"The Enfield was OK, but throughout the '60s and '70s I went to Ted's Café on Eastern Avenue and saw lots of faster bikes. I bought bits, assembled a Norton Dominator café racer in my council flat. I fired it up to test the motor, then took the back wheel out, heaved it into the lift to get it downstairs for its debut road test."

Anthony recalled the Rocker scene then was almost becoming an underground thing.

"There was still this image that Rockers, or Greasers as they began to be called in the early '70s, were

Anthony and his Matchless P11 in East London. Note the graffiti and neglected buildings, typical of '70s Britain.

Anthony Curzon and pillion passenger test ride their Norton café racer in the '70s.

troublemakers. Few places would let you in if you had your Pride & Clarke leathers on. I went to the Brighton Motorcycle Show in '69 and had cups thrown at me from the roadside."

Anthony remembered the bikes still inextricably linked with '50s rock 'n' roll.

"I went to the Fishmongers Arms on Saturday nights to see the rock 'n' roll bands – Shakin' Stevens started out there. The Rising Sun at Walthamstow was another place where the original Rockers went. The times were exciting then. I used to roadie a bit for Screamin' Lord Sutch, what a character he was – I had to wait in the wings and rush on stage to put things out when he set them on fire."

Most of all, having a café racer Norton Dominator, the leather gear and a love for rock 'n' roll was a ticket to some good times.

"I just had to have a big bike, as the Enfield Crusader got blown to the weeds by a Yamaha 250. The cafés, the runs to Southend or Brighton in the summer ... God I miss those days.

"We had a mate called Kelvin, but everyone called him Jinxy. He rode pillion all the time as he had no bike, but nearly everyone who ferried him about had a crash. Ironically, Jinxy's dad was a traffic cop with the London Met, and I think his dad actually went to an accident one day and found his son battered and bruised by the roadside. It was inevitable really."

Pete Coombs aboard his Bonneville 650 café racer in 1973.

Pete Coombs also spent the '60s on various bikes, with the Busy Bee being his local haunt.

"It was a seven mile ride from Harrow to the Bee, just enough for me," remembered Pete. "People would bomb along the A41 outside the Bee, speed-testing. Occasionally, some joker would ride his bike through one door and out of the other."

Pete owned a Triumph 500 twin, but bought himself a 1969 Bonneville 650 café racer in the early '70s.

"I think that bike had been a proddie racer or something, it didn't half go. All the kit on it, clip-ons, rear sets, and someone had removed the tank badges so they didn't get broken when the handlebars were on full lock. I remember that by the mid-'70s café racers were getting hard to sell, the values really dropped off, especially on British stuff."

Thirteen Gold Stars and a supermodel wife

As the values of British bikes slipped, Pete Schneider, a young biker in the Midlands, indulged his passion for BSA Gold Star singles.

"My first bike was a BSA C15 I rebuilt in my garage, but I really loved Gold Stars. At one stage I owned thirteen Goldies," said Pete, "and I don't think I paid more than £250 for any of 'em. People virtually gave them away in the '70s."

But although Pete fettled his Goldies, he also built himself a Norvelo café racer, and it ended up bringing him some luck with the ladies.

"I put a Velocette 500 engine inside a Featherbed frame, and found that the megaphone exhaust I fitted was a bit loud. So I fabricated my own silencer flap, ran a cable to it from the 'bars. That meant I could keep

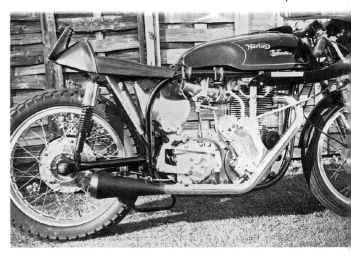

You can just see the handy exhaust flap, activated by a cable running from the handlebars, which Pete made to keep his Velo-engined café racer quiet in town.

Pete recalled Chrissy from school, who "took a very good photo," and he persuaded her to model for *Motorcycle World* magazine in the '70s.

it quiet in town, then open it up when I was out of the speed limits."

Pete's Norvelo ran bigger valves in the engine, TT100 tyres and a finned fuel intake chamber to keep the fuel cooler before it went in the cylinder. It was one of many British bikes he built for fun.

"I built a Gold Star special and sent a picture to *Motorcycle World* magazine in the USA. It had a '30s BSA Gold Star all-aluminium engine in it, pretty rare, so they wanted to do a feature on it.

"The mag wrote to me and suggested I get a pretty girl to model on the bike for the pictures, so I was walking down the street one day and saw this photo of a nice-looking girl in a photographer's shop window. I remembered her, it was Christine from school.

"So I tracked her down, got her to do the photo shoot, chatted her up – and ended up marrying her. But

I'll tell you what, I don't think she's been on a motorbike since that day!"

When BSA went bust in the early '70s, Pete hung onto his Gold Star collection throughout the decade, breaking the bikes into parts and storing them in tea chests for nearly 20 years. But it wasn't as hard as he expected to find parts to re-commission his Goldies in the '90s.

"Len Vale-Onslow proved to be brilliant." said Pete, "I went to the shop one day in the '90s and asked 'young' Len, who was about 60-odd then, if he had some spare valves. I him showed one, and young Len called his Dad to the counter. At the time Len senior must have been

A Gold Star 350 engine, RR T2 gearbox and a bigger GP carb make this one of Pete's favourite Goldies from his motorcycling past – he's owned 13 of the big BSA singles.

over 90, but he recognised the valves as being from a 1938 Gold Star 350 immediately. What was even better was that he had brand new, boxed-up spares, plus gasket sets, pistons – everything."

Pete used the parts to make a Goldie 350 café racer, housing the 1930s single-cylinder engine in a Manx Norton frame and using an RRT2 gearbox. He still rides it to this day, alongside a Hailwood Rep Ducati 900SS, which 'Mike the Bike' actually sold to Pete back in 1980.

"Mike Hailwood was one of my heroes because he was so ordinary, he raced for the fun of it. I was at the 13th milestone in 1978 when Read broke down on the Honda, and as Mike came past on the final lap he took his hand off the 'bars and flicked the V-sign at Phil. That was Mike all over, anything for a bit of a laugh."

Sticking with specials

John Hartas in Darlington began riding in the '50s on a Velocette MAC 350, graduating to a Triumph Tiger 110. His local café was at Charter Hall in the Scottish Borders, where he used to wait in lay-bys for someone to come past, then dice with them on the undulating A-roads.

John went on holiday in the '60s to Gloucestershire, saw a Triton café racer in a dealer's window, and bought it on the spot.

"It had an open primary chain case and we had to keep stopping to lube the chain whilst I carried on my holiday. When I got home my dad persuaded me to strip it down. We put 9:1 pistons in it, did the timing properly and it flew! I owned that bike for over 25 years, commuted to work on it – didn't own a car until the '70s. Lovely thing it was – I sold it to a mate and he put a 650SS Norton motor in it in the '90s and restored the bike."

Pete on his Norton-Velo special, ready for a ride in the '70s.

John Hartas getting the feel of his Triton back in the '60s.

Like many riders, Ralph inherited a love of motorcycles from his dad, seen here in northern England in the late '30s.

Eve Pilkington takes a break back in the early '60s aboard Ralph's BSA/Tiger Cub hybrid, built from £15 worth of bits.

Ralph Pilkington's Dunstall Triton from the '60s, with wife Eve and baby daughter admiring the handiwork.

Ralph Pilkington of Lancashire also stuck with his own modified bikes.

"I started out in the '50s with a 'bitsa' I made for fun," said Ralph. "It had a BSA Bantam engine in a Tiger Cub frame, Bantam forks as well, plus a Ducati fuel tank – the whole thing cost me just £15. I kept tweaking and changing it over the years."

Ralph got to know John Tickle at Unity Equipe in the early '60s, who had bought the rights to make the Manx Norton singles.

"John and his staff knew bikes inside out," recalled Ralph, "so when I fancied building a Triton I contacted Unity, got loads of bits made by them, advice and so on. The real stroke of luck I had when building my Triton was contacting Dunstall for a fairing and exhaust pipes. They had a couple of nine-stud cylinder heads, all gas-flowed ready for racing, so I got those at a good price too."

Local places that Ralph and his wife Eve (pictured) went to back in the '60s included Hollingworth Lake near Rochdale, and the Roundhouse café.

"I used to pal around with a bloke called Jeff Grimes in the early '60s. He had a Tiger 110, which was a fast machine, but sadly died just three days after I took a photo of him sat on the bike. Some good people are missed from those days, as well as the cafés and the bikes."

Endless summer of '59

The 59 Club developed rapidly in the '60s, becoming the biggest motorcycle club in the world with over 30,000 members. It also has strong connections with the Ace Café. Father Bill Shergold, who was working with Reverend John Oates at a youth club in Hackney, London in the early '60s, decided he would try and reach out to the youngsters branded as 'troublemakers' by the tabloid press of the time.

Father Bill famously recalled later that he "rode past the Ace a couple of times and didn't stop, I was so nervous." But once inside he made friends and the 59 Club was founded in Hackney, rapidly gaining celebrity status after Bill's work with motorcyclists made the national press. Giles, the *Daily Express* cartoonist captured Bill as the 'Ton-up vicar'.

Bill Shergold left London in the '60s, starting the 69 Club in Dover, and later retiring to the West Country. In the late '60s, the 59 Club moved to Paddington. Del Hooper recalled his days, and nights, spent there.

"Because it was run by the church, the 59 Club had respectability, but more importantly it had a real credibility with the youth of the '60s and '70s. It was a place where you were welcome with a black leather jacket on – that was rare at the time."

Del recalled that the 59 Club in Paddington had a lively social scene that went way beyond a shared interest in motorcycling.

"Saturday nights, when there was a dance on, over 1000 people would turn up. Local character Little Ray would be on the door, loads of bikes outside, you could hear people stamping upstairs in time to the music. Great atmosphere."

The era was famous for its clashes between Mods and Rockers, but Del reckoned these were few and far between.

"Generally, there was very little trouble, but it happened. A mate of mine went to Brighton and got a bit of a pasting from some Mods, then arrested. His brother was in the police and luckily got him out, but he was set upon again – and arrested again. This time he was charged and next day when him and his mates saw an unfortunate Mod chained to a lamp-post, well, they couldn't resist a bit of payback ..."

One of the lynchpins of the 59 Club was Mike Cook.

"The 59 Club was my life for over 30 years," recalled Mike. "Back in the early '60s I worked in London and went to the Ace Café, and other places on my bike. I joined the 59 Club one Saturday night and a few months later it struck me that the card index membership system was a bit inefficient. Like a fool, I suggested it could be improved – next thing I'd been roped in to help out."

Mike graduated from his Royal Enfield Meteor Minor to a BSA Super Rocket 650 in the '60s. He also dressed up as a medieval knight in armour for a BBC 2 TV show, scaled 70-foot ladders to fix the clubhouse roof, and picked up some speeding endorsements on his BSA.

"I suppose I wasn't setting too good an example with the speeding," remembered Mike, "but at least it gave me some credibility with the fast lads who visited the club."

The 59 Club wasn't a place of outright youth rebellion, as it had to provide an annual report for the local education authority, justifying the money spent on reaching out to the youth of the day. It had to be seen to be doing good, but keep the more rebellious motorcyclists interested, too.

"It was a fine line," said Mike Cook, "and we did it by doing things like showing *The Wild One* in the late '60s. This iconic '50s film, starring Marlon Brando and

(continued page 35)

The Tahiti in Leamington Spa in 1967. (Courtesy The Mike Cook Collection)

This night shot at Chelsea Bridge in the '60s shows a typical Friday night crowd. (Courtesy The Mike Cook Collection)

The Cellar café, at Windsor in Berkshire. (Courtesy The Mike Cook Collection)

Lee Marvin, was banned in Britain for well over a decade, and I think the 59 Club was one of the first organisations to screen it. The club was packed that night, people queued up outside, and we had to show it again the following night. You look back at the film now and you wonder why the authorities made such a fuss about it really."

As each generation of new riders came along, the 59 Club kept growing.

"The club was a good influence on many young riders," said Mike. "When we moved to Hackney in '74 there were lots of 16 year olds getting mopeds and racing around the estates. The 59 Club was a place they could go, learn how to fix up their bikes. It was difficult for the kids, because lots of the older riders in those days, who owned larger motorcycles, didn't want anything to do with the moped riders.

"Looking back, the 59 Club provided a welcome for anyone on two wheels, and that's the heart of its fundamental appeal, the reason why it's one of the biggest motorcycle clubs in the world."

The 59 Club is still thriving today, based in Plaistow, East London, and retains its spirit of down-to-earth friendliness.

Mike Cook (left) interviews Derek, owner of the Tahiti in Leamington, in the mid-'60s. (Courtesy The Mike Cook Collection)

Mike Cook travelled to Squires café in the winter of 1965 to do a feature for the 59 Club magazine on this famous Yorkshire meeting point for motorcyclists. (Courtesy The Mike Cook Collection)

Factory rides and bolt-on goodies

Throughout the '60s and '70s, the big players like Dunstall, Rickman and Colin Seeley all made chassis kits, complete bikes, or tuning parts for over-500cc machines, but it was left to smaller companies, and some enterprising bike dealers, to offer café racer goodies for the popular 250-400cc class machinery of the '70s.

Young riders in the UK then could ride a 250cc bike on a learner licence, and many wanted to tune-up or customise their Japanese bikes. Mead Speed and Mel le Moto offered a variety of parts for Yamaha models. Apple, and Sanders & Lewis specialised in Suzuki, whilst Dixon Racing and Read Titan offered 'kitted-up' Hondas, like the Dixon Racing 400/4 featuring a 460cc engine.

On the surface, it seemed that the Japanese bike makers were repeating the mistakes of the British manufacturers, and ignoring the demand from younger riders of the '70s for 'go-faster' specials in the smaller capacity market. But Paul Dunstall recalls that the Japanese saw things differently.

"We worked with Yamaha Europe about doing stuff for the RD range, and they wanted to do it, plus they would warranty the bikes via their dealer network. But Yamaha Japan had an issue with liability – they were worried that if someone got killed on a Dunstall-accessorised Yamaha, the press would have a go at them.

"Honda and Suzuki felt much the same, which is why you had Rickman-, Seeley- or Dunstall-branded machines using Japanese engines, electrics, etc. They all wanted just a bit of distance between themselves and any tricked-up bikes.

"Honda were lovely to work with, very open. I was allowed free access to their experimental shop

Dunstall made this fairing and matching bodywork for the Yamaha RD350 and XS500 models in 1976.

Dunstall had an offer to become an official Honda accessory and tuning house in the late '70s.

over in California. We built a special CB750 for Honda to evaluate and they also wanted us to design a complete seat/tank/panel unit for the Superdream 250/400 models, similar to the bigger bikes."

That never happened, although Paul Dunstall could have become much closer to Honda in the '70s.

"By the end of the '70s, I was getting bored with the bike industry," recalled Paul. "Things were tough, I was laying people off, and I didn't like that. I was approached by Honda USA to be a Honda-authorised tuning house, in the same way that AMG is associated with Mercedes. The offer was very generous. In fact, Honda USA simply asked me to name my price."

But Paul was already moving into the property market and felt that he might be a cog in Honda's wheel.

"In the end, I liked to work alone, go my own way. I didn't want to end up doing corporate things for Honda."

Britain fades into a rising sun

The British bike industry did try to join in with the café racer boom.

Triumph made the Thruxton Bonneville in the mid-'60s, to capitalise on its success in the annual endurance race held at the circuit. Norton made the JPS 850 Commando Production race rep of the early '70s, after success with Peter Williams.

"Peter was always trying new things," recalled Dave Croxford, "and his bikes were set up so well. He was

The limited edition John Player Norton Commando was one of the last attempts by the 'old' British bike industry to produce a café racer.

The Royal Enfield Continental 250 GT had all the right gear. Single seat, clip-ons, long fuel tank, 'bacon-slicer' front brake – but a modest 21bhp motor.

great at development work – I just raced 'em. I could take a gearbox to bits and fix it, but Peter could tell you how it worked, how power was transmitted through the different ratios. Clever bloke, knew his chassis design as well – he invented the cast alloy wheel."

But in general, British café racers were cosmetic exercises – standard models, decked out with bolt-on goodies. Dealers were frequently used for machine development, and one notable example of this is Gander and Gray's involvement with the Royal Enfield Continental GT 250 – arguably the only true factory café racer from the old British bike industry.

Based on the humble Crusader 250, the Continental GT appeared in 1966 and featured clip-ons, tacho, crankcase breather pipe, fly screen, rear sets, single seat and an elongated fuel tank. Gander and Gray also had an exclusive deal with Royal Enfield, supplying even more goodies for this cute coffee bar racer.

Others tried adding café style. AJS jazzed up its big twin range with the 650 CSR, after repeated requests from its US distributor for a 'go-faster' model. For a good decade or so, there was a rivalry between fans of British and Japanese bikes, and plenty of riders stuck with British iron.

Malcolm Powell got hooked on bikes in the '70s and owned a BSA A10 café racer.

"I bought a café racer secretly and stored it at Baz's place, it was beautiful. An A10 Road Rocket with flat bars, swept back pipes, fibreglass tank and seat unit, plus a lot of chrome and brass fittings. I spent lots of time and money totally rebuilding that A10, painting it black and gold, renewing engine parts. It was a good bike, but I was at the Swan pub one day in the West Country and I saw an unusual bike. That was the beginning of my love affair with Ducatis."

Malc Powell's mate Rich poses with his Trident T160, later featuring a mural of Che Guevara on the fuel tank, plus Malcolm's BSA A10 café racer.

Malcolm 'Cozy' Powell, next to his mate Baz's Norton café racer, when the gang was on its way to Devon for a summer holiday.

The Italian job

Some might argue that the Italians invented the world's second oldest profession, road racing. The nation has a passion for competition and improving the performance of anything with an engine. Its road bikes often reflect this obsession with competition.

In the late '60s, Moto Guzzi, Benelli, MV Agusta and Ducati were tooling up to make big, road-based motorcycles to compete with the British, German and Japanese brands. Ducati approached Colin Seeley who met with Fabio Taglioni in October 1970 and agreed to build a short run of racing chassis for Ducati's 500- and 750-sized race projects.

Each chassis cost Ducati just £125 apiece, surely

The beautiful Ducati 750S, exotic back in the '70s; a sought-after classic street-racer today.

Another rare beauty, the Ducati 750SS from the mid-'70s, made in limited numbers to help Ducati qualify for various production racing series.

This Seeley MkIII chassis inspired the Italian Ducati company to commission Colin Seeley to produce a racing frame for it in the early '70s. Note the Moto Martin CBX in the background at this Festival of 1000 Bikes meeting.

one of the great bargains in motorcycle development, especially as that chassis became the basis for the famous '72 Imola 200 race-winner, ridden by Bruno Spaggiari and Paul Smart.

Ducati wasted little time in getting a road version of the Imola 200 racer into production. The 750S and SS models, alongside the later 900SS, are motorcycles that capture the very essence of the '70s factory café racer. Long fuel tank, clip-ons, a sparse tubular frame, using the engine as a stressed member, and a pair of upswept Conti silencers give the '70s Ducati a café credibility – it's a genuinely sporty machine, straight from the factory, no tweaking required.

The 750SS had a V-twin rival, in the shape of the Moto Guzzi 750 S3, which later became the beautiful Le Mans 850 of '76, another iconic bike of its time. Unlike Ducati, Guzzi had no racing cachet to help sell the Le Mans, but the sexy, rakish looks and grunty power won over plenty of riders.

The Guzzi Le Mans was one of the most popular factory café racers of the '70s. This is the MkII Le Mans in action at Mallory Park.

The logical conclusion for Italian enthusiasts in the '70s was a company making nothing but road legal specials. A beautiful chassis, hand-made engineering details, and the best available engines. The company that filled that gap was Bimota, which – after a distinctly rocky road – is still in business today.

Mail order specials

"My first bike was a Suzuki AP50," recalls Steve 'Carpy' Carpenter, CB750 specials-builder born in London, "which I rode illegally, then I got done by the police, just after turning 16, for riding it with no pedals fitted. You couldn't have a sports moped then with the pedals still on it – that was ****ing blasphemy!"

Riders like Celia Powell could accessorise their Honda 400/4 with coloured fork gaiters, Ace 'bars and a special Alfa exhaust system.

replaced wide handlebars on an RD400 with Ace 'bars, or a scraped seat unit with a Sondel Sport item."

The motorcycle press in the UK carried large classified sections, where owners could choose from a vast array of tuning parts, exhausts, chassis tweaks like steering dampers, fork braces, stiffer shock absorbers, etc.

There were plenty of companies making racy-looking bodywork for a variety of bikes. Dyson Originals sold futuristic body styling kits for the Kawasaki two-stroke triples, and used the Bol d'Or group of dealers in Eastern England to retail them. Flow Line Fabrications made a Heron Suzuki race team painted kit for the Suzuki X7 250, whilst Mel le Moto, Sondel Sport and Ham Yam Racing all had success with body kits for the Yamaha RD series.

Built for comfort and speed

When it came to bigger Japanese bikes, Dunstall and Rickman dominated the aftermarket fairing and bodywork scene in the '70s. Paul Dunstall started with the Suzuki GT500, then made sports and touring fairings for the Honda CB500/750 fours, Kawasaki Z1 and Suzuki's GT750. Dunstall even diversified and tried a sports fairing kit for the BMW R75 and R90 twins, plus matching clubman handlebars.

"We also produced a universal nose fairing," remembers Paul Dunstall, "which could be used without changing the handlebars on most bikes. It was aimed at those who just wanted a simple addition to their bike."

The younger generation who started motorcycling in the '70s began on the small capacity Japanese mopeds, or 125cc-250cc machinery. The bikes were fast, but there were plenty of dealers, distributors and manufacturers who could make them look or go even faster.

"Doing your bike up was necessary then," agrees Eamon Maloney, now a café racer collector, "mainly because half of us kept slinging them up the road and we couldn't afford stock parts to repair them. So you

Rickman was at its peak in the late '70s, when most new motorcycles didn't feature any weather protection as standard.

The Rickman CRE 1000 Kawasaki took its inspiration from the endurance racers of the time, but was actually more of a tourer than a sports bike.

Rickman's most famous rolling chassis bikes from the era were undoubtedly the CR750 Honda and CR1000 Kawasaki kits – the Kawasaki cost just £590.00 back in 1975 when it was launched. Rickman exported thousands of chassis kits, featuring Lockheed brakes, Spanish Betor forks and the Reynolds 531 tubular frame. Aside from making complete bikes, Don and Derek also struck a deal with Honda in '76 to make the Hondastyle range of fairings and luggage.

Rickman's mid-'70s CR750 and CR1000 bikes truly defined the era, in terms of styling, performance and sales success. Rickman sold over 12,000 bikes in the '70s, many going abroad to the USA, Australia, Germany, etc., as the café racer craze caught on.

But Rickman had competition. Colin Seeley took a racer's scalpel to the CB750 Honda in 1975, and housed a smooth, 1000cc Honda engine in a lightweight chassis. The bike attracted interest and led to Seeley being commissioned to make a Phil Read replica for 1978, after Phil won the 1977 F1 TT race on a Honda.

Years later, Eamon Maloney spoke to Gerald Davidson, then boss of Honda UK, who was in charge of the project and saw an opportunity missed.

The Phil Read replica CB750 Honda looked great, but lacked the genuine Seeley touch.

A year later the Phil Read replica had become the Honda Britain 750SS.

"Gerald said Honda's F2 model 750 was being trounced by the new GS750 Suzuki," recalled Eamon, "so the Phil Read replica was a marketing fix, to shift unsold units of the latest 750. That's why they never used Colin Seeley's chassis."

The project hit further problems after Phil Read asked for his promised royalties on every bike sold, and didn't receive anything. So the following year the bike was rebranded as the Honda Britain 750SS, and painted in white rather than red.

Bad girls and wicked 'Elsies'

Although the '70s saw pioneering attempts to tame the superbike engines of the time, few succeeded as sporting road bikes. They were just too heavy. Smaller, lighter machines, like the RD400 and RD350LC (affectionately known as the 'Elsie') handled and braked so well, that with some mild tweaking it was possible to build a giant-killer of a special.

There were plenty of specialists and aftermarket suppliers waiting to help. Stan Stephens and Terry Shepherd were renowned engine-tuners, Allspeed made expansion chamber exhausts, whilst a host of companies offered everything from a Telefix fork brace to a set of Kenny Roberts replica bodywork.

"I used to hang around Matlock Bath in Derbyshire back in the '80s. Some, including myself, used to race

Mitch and her RD350LC, plus '80s Ford Capri.

Mitch on her street racer RD350LC, which she still owns today. Note the paddock jacket and cowboy boots – typical riding kit for the '80s.

Girl biker Mitch Curran in the '80s, on her RD250LC.

from Matlock to Whatstandwell Bridge where the actual bridge acted as a chicane. People used to sit on the bridge and see who leaned their bikes over the most. I preferred to set off from Matlock Bath traffic lights in full view of everyone and pull power wheelies – wicked power band on the LC!"

Mitch still owns an RD350LC today, which was one of the cult bikes of the '80s. She modified her LC with Aeroquip brake lines, Metmachex swingarm, engine tuning by Stan Stephens and rear sets by Mel le Moto. Mitch rode around with her friend Shirley, and often visited Darley Moor race circuit to watch the production races there.

"It was dodge the sheep whilst spectating back then," remembered Mitch, "but the racing was always full-on, head banging stuff. Inspired us to ride to pubs like the Anchor at Oakerothorpe in Derbyshire – still a great bikers pub today."

Race from the crate

During the early '80s, an economic recession, plus the ever-improving Japanese sport bikes, began to squeeze the specialists out.

Paul Dunstall quit the industry, Rickman diversified and marketed a kind of low budget Jeep called the Ranger. Georges Martin, founder of Moto Martin, ventured into kit cars. The scene was changing. Many riders in Europe didn't have the money to extensively modify, or build their own specials, and the motorway network was picking off the old A-road cafés one by one, as UK towns and cities became bypassed.

Bikes like the GSXR750 and Honda RC30 demonstrated that the Japanese had been patiently learning from the British chassis specialists like Seeley, Harris, Peckett & McNab, and other overseas builders like JJ Cobas, Bakker and Bimota. Fuel injection, turbocharging and electronic ignitions began to move mainstream motorcycles beyond the reach of many home mechanics.

The job of building modern specials was becoming exclusive to professionals like Harris, Bimota, Moko, Tony Foale, Ikuzawa, Britten, etc. All that was left for the amateur on a tight budget was a selection of British bikes, but that suited enthusiasts like Les Emery, who wanted to refine and develop the Norton Dominator and Commando into a practical, fast classic bike.

But the days of retailing thousands of rolling chassis, big bore kits, and more, had come to an end. For a while, it looked like the café racer was fading into history.

Suzuki's GSXR750, launched in 1985, was a sportbike you could simply race straight from the crate, or ride fast on the road. The 1100 GSXR engine would also fit in easily, should you decide to add some extra power. It was the factory café racer, at an affordable price.

Paul Emery with the Marigold Motorcycles Norton racer, ridden by Mike Shoesmith in the '80s. Paul's father, Les, founded the Norvil Motorcycle Company later in the '80s.

The specialists

At first, riders began to customise their own machines, but, as the '60s progressed, an alternative motorcycle industry developed, as demand for café racer-style extras, or complete bikes, increased.

Overseas markets like the USA, Australia and mainland Europe followed this fashion, providing a springboard for bigger companies like Dunstall and Rickman to establish substantial production lines, manufacturing both complete bikes and a variety of hard parts and accessories.

But between the big boys and the home-builder, there were myriad specialists, importers of particular go-faster products, and small-scale manufacturers of everything from fairings to footrests, Ace 'bars to exhausts.

This chapter has an A-Z listing of some of the more influential names in the British café racer boom, but it's not comprehensive, so apologies to anyone missed out.

Anglo Bike

Pete Frost formed Anglo Bike in the late '70s, inspired by the success of the Rob North-framed Triumph Tridents of the late '60s/early '70s.

Using nickel-plated, T45 tubing, Anglo Bike created bespoke frame kits and complete bikes for those who still clung to Brit bike culture, when everyone else was busy signing HP agreements to buy a new Honda CB750 or Kawasaki Z1.

Anglo Bike used Betor forks, Lockheed discs and Girling shocks on its Tristar showpiece machines. These accepted either the T140 Bonneville or T150/160 series Trident engines, and a rolling chassis cost a hefty £1995

Anglo Bike offered the Tristar and Thruxton as track machines, or street legal café racers.

for the Trident in the late '70s – nearly twice as much as the original T160 cost brand-new in the mid '70s.

Dresda Autos

Dave Degens famously bought Dresda Autos, a former scooter shop, in 1963, when the bottom fell out of the scooter boom at exactly the same moment he was

Dave Degens reunited with a 'Moto-Ball' competition prize, Dresda Honda special, which he created for the motorcycling newspaper *MCN* back in 1980.
(Courtesy Steve and Nirvana Motorcycles UK)

looking to establish his own business as a builder of Tritons.

Like many improvers on standard British motorcycles of the '50s and '60s, Degens learned his craft via the racetrack. He raced AJS, BSA and Triton machines, quickly learning what worked, and what didn't, then applied those basic engineering lessons on his bikes.

The true stroke of genius Degens pulled off was in designing a kind of template for the Triton. Degens placed the engine as far forward in the Norton frame as possible, rubber-mounted the carbs and fibre-glass gas tank to lessen vibration, and fitted a potent front brake.

Dave also tweaked the Triumph 650 Bonneville engines, fitting 3134 cams and 32mm Amal carbs, balancing the crankshafts, and installing high-compression pistons. He also worked hard on making engine plates that allowed the drivechain to run arrow-straight.

His work was a clever, precisely assembled, race-tested refinement of both the Triumph motor and the Norton chassis. That attention to detail gave the Dresda Triton a discernible edge.

Degens' most famous race was the 1965 Barcelona 24-hour Endurance, which he won on his own Triton. He went back to Barcelona in 1969 and won again. He also devised a box-section swinging arm and an improved swinging arm pivot assembly, both for Yamaha race machines, in the late '60s.

The Dresda box-section swinging arm went on to become an almost compulsory fitment for many '70s specials, but as Degens later modestly told *Bike* magazine in the '80s: "The box section swinging arm offered no real engineering advantage, it just looked trick."

By the late '60s the Triton boom was coming to end, mainly because the supply of cheap Featherbed frames was drying up. Degens began designing his own Dresda chassis from scratch using Reynolds tubing, and promptly won a couple of races. He later added a monoshock rear end to his frame.

At its height in the '70s, Dresda Autos had two shops, one at Putney and another at Isleworth, offering complete rolling chassis for bikes such as the Suzuki GT750 two-stroke or Kawasaki Z1, with modern touches such as cast magnesium wheels. Dave also

This is the Blinking Owl Café at Southend in the late '60s. Note that most riders weren't wearing helmets, which were not compulsory then, or much protective riding gear at all. (Courtesy The Mike Cook Collection)

worked closely with French Honda importer Japauto, designing a frame for its endurance racing CB750 Honda machines.

By the '80s, the Japanese manufacturers were learning how to make their bikes handle a bit better.

They took a step back from their close association with specialist frame-builders and chassis developers. Degens re-launched his Triton business in the mid '80s and continues to offer his own unique take on the Triton concept well into the 21st century.

Paul Dunstall

Paul Dunstall said he "reversed into the motorcycle aftermarket industry, almost by accident."

As a teenager in the 1950s, Paul ran a scooter shop in Eltham, South London and made enough money to buy himself a Norton Dominator. After burning off a few guys on the road, 18-year-old Paul went road racing and then began to search for ways to make his Dommie quicker.

"I had a bloke bend some pipes for me, making them fit closer to the engine and upswept, to improve ground clearance. I took a guess on the design of the megaphone pipes as regards improving power – as it turned out, I guessed correctly," recalled Paul.

Having had six pairs of pipes made in case of crashes, Paul hung the exhausts in his shop, and found motorcycle riders started asking to buy them. Suddenly Paul Dunstall was in the aftermarket business and he quit racing, sponsoring his mate Fred Neville, then later Ray Pickrell, as his Dunstall-Norton riders and testing engine tuning mods, brakes and exhausts on the track before selling them.

Paul was also quick to pick up on Colin Lyster's early disc brake success with Dave Croxford, Phil Read and others, offering a Dunstall single or twin front disc setup on his tweaked Atlas and Commando models.

Like Dave Degens at Dresda, Paul Dunstall entered his specially built bikes in production class road racing events in 1967, knowing it would stir up controversy, which helped spread the Dunstall name. In fact, the Dunstall Nortons of the era were registered and taxed as being road legal, production motorbikes.

When the Japanese companies began making larger bikes, Paul Dunstall could see an opportunity.

"I was already exporting a fair bit, so the Dunstall name was known," said Paul, "We worked with Yamaha in Holland,

A fully 'Dunstallized' Suzuki GS1000, offered for the '78 riding season.

The Kawasaki Z900 or Z1000 could be transformed into a kind of endurance racer by Paul Dunstall.

Honda and Kawasaki USA, Mitsui Yamaha and Heron Suzuki in the UK. I don't think they wanted to be left out, just in case the café racer trend really became big news."

The Dunstall CB750, Kawasaki Z1, and most famously the Suzuki GS1000 and GSX1100 models all set high speeds in road tests of the time, exceeding 150mph in the case of the Suzuki.

But times changed, and by the early '80s Paul could see an economic recession taking its toll on his bike business.

"At one stage my accountants were telling me I was earning too much from the Dunstall Organisation, then ten years later, we were struggling. As I'd started to make money in the UK property market I decided to quit the bike industry in the '80s. I have no interest in owning a classic motorbike, as modern ones are so fantastic – better than anything we could have dreamed about back in the '50s."

The staid Yamaha XS500 could be spruced up with a sports fairing, clip-ons, front mudguard and rear sets.

Ian Dyson

Inspired by the 'drop over' bodywork kits that Paul Dunstall made popular in the '70s for the big Japanese machines, Ian Dyson tried the same approach with smaller, 250cc-400cc-sized bikes.

Ian Dyson Originals was based in Yorkshire, and designed futuristic kits for the Kawasaki KH250 and KH400 models of the mid-'70s. Later on, Dyson expanded into designing extras for the RD250/350LC series, but the '80s recession and the 125cc learner law, which effectively killed the 250 market in Britain overnight, put Dyson out of business.

Fritz Egli

Swiss designer Egli began his frame-tweaking activities due to his racing Vincent's handling problems. Egli sat down in the late '60s and redesigned the Vincent frame completely, immediately winning races with his new tubular spine, cantilevered rear end design.

The strength, the sheer 'rightness' of this design was such that Egli influenced later chassis-builders like Tony Foale, Moko and Moto Martin. In the 21st century, the French-made Godet-Egli Vincent café racers keep the design alive.

In the '90s, Egli became the Swiss importer for Indian-made Royal Enfield motorcycles, and set about working his magic on those '50s-designed classics.

Tony Foale

A qualified nuclear engineer, Tony Foale grew up in Australia, and came to Britain in the mid-1970s after Steve Parrish won an F750 race on a Foale-framed TZ750 Yamaha.

Foale drew inspiration from Fritz Egli, as his chassis featured a thick steel tube spine, suspending the engine from it, with a triangulated, cantilever rear end, featuring a de Carbon monoshock – Foale was the UK importer for de Carbon at the time.

In the '80s, Foale advanced the cause of the hub-centre-steered motorcycle frame with his Quantum project. Basically, Foale wanted to do away with telescopic forks and the cradle frame. His ideas provoked debate, but never really caught on, and, despite Yamaha's application of hub-centre steering on its GTS1000, we remain stuck with telescopic forks.

Harris Performance

Steve and Lester Harris raced British bikes in the '60s, forming opinions on how things could be improved as they diced. In 1970 they made a replacement Featherbed frame for their own Triton project, then a beautiful Seeley-like, cantilevered monoshock chassis for a Suzuki 250 racer.

Orders from fellow road racers came in, so in 1972 the pair formed Harris Performance Products. Over the next two decades Harris became one of the most influential frame-makers in the UK, and, in the world of GP racing, provided expertise for Barry Sheene's factory Suzuki and Yamaha 500s.

But Harris didn't neglect the grass roots riders, and its mid-'70s endurance racing trellis frame became the famous Magnum design, a benchmark rolling chassis kit for many street-specials builders of the '80s.

Although Harris produced hi-tech, alloy twin beam frames from the mid-'80s onward, and worked on the Sauber/Petronas GP project in the late '90s, it always remained keen on tubular construction.

In the '80s, Harris made frames for the Ikuzawa Honda singles, and worked closely with Norman Hyde on the Harrier and Hornet Triumph projects. It continues to work with Norman Hyde on the Hinckley-engined Harriers to the present day.

Norman Hyde

Norman Hyde worked at Triumph Meriden for many years, starting as an apprentice in the '60s. A keen sprinter, Norman set several speed records in the '60s. His wife, Diana, accompanied him at over 120mph as a sidecar passenger in his supercharged 350 T90 outfit, wearing deck shoes with her racing leathers!

"I got into the experimental department, which was much more interesting than the production line," remembered Norman. "Percy Tait used to roar in, park the bike, leave hurriedly and the police would arrive ... we would look at this bike with its engine tinkling away and say 'Who? Test rider? No, we haven't seen anyone ...' It was a regular occurrence with Percy."

Norman recalled the café scene of the Midlands at that time was pretty lively.

"There was a café in Warwick, the El Ciente I think. Guys with Gold Stars used to set off together, all with open meggas on – there was a kind of doppler effect ... not so enjoyable for the residents I imagine. The New Yorker at Leamington was another place we all used to go to – many lads did the classic thing of putting a record on and trying to race around a few local roads before it finished."

After the Norton Villiers Triumph group finally collapsed in the late '70s, Norman established his own business making a range of products for British triples and twins, before launching the Harrier Trident in the '80s.

The bike featured a bored out 850cc engine, which later grew to a full 1000cc triple. The Harris brothers

Norman Hyde back in his drag-racing days on a twin-engined Trident.

Norman Hyde in his workshop today.

The '80s Harrier T160 was a well-engineered update on a British classic from the '70s.

end shells as hinges. We initiated him into the world of Birmingham strip clubs – I don't think he'd seen anything like it." recalled Norman.

Having spent the latter years of the 20th century making specials based around the Trident and Bonneville, plus the Toga exhaust brand, Norman decided to revive the Harrier in the 21st century, utilising the Hinckley Bonneville twin.

"The new Harrier has a Harris frame, you can't go wrong with Steve and Lester, plus bodywork by Asa Moyce and optional Ohlins suspension. We might do a chassis for the triples, it depends on what Triumph themselves do, of course."

Norman still thinks that road racing will always inspire new riders, however. "Lots of modern bike builders forget development, they think that a computer program will tell you all you need to know, but you will have to go racing to find out if something really is faster, or better handling, than the old model."

designed the chassis, which was based on a vision of what a Rob North T180 Trident might have looked like, had NVT stayed in business another five years or so. Italian Marzocchi suspension, Astralite wheels and Lockheed brakes made it a classy café racer, fusing the old and new with a certain elan.

Later in the '80s, Norman went racing with a Hyde Bonneville in the US Bears twin-cylinder series, with Geoff Johnson as their sponsored rider.

"Geoff was great to have around, he fitted the gates to my workshop actually, using old Meriden factory big-

Mead Speed
Based in Newport Pagnell, Mead Speed was a Yamaha specialist, offering kitted-up two stroke specials in the '70s and '80s. Like many others, it offered parts like full fairings, rear sets, clip-ons, etc., to owners of road going Yamahas and smaller Kawasaki and Suzuki two-strokes.

Mel Le Moto
A mail-order purveyor of Yamaha goodies, Mel Le Moto offered a wide selection of bolt-on bits, especially rear sets, plus created fully-faired, TZ-styled RD250/350 street specials in the '70s.

Moto Martin

The French Moto Martin custom house offered Egli-style rolling chassis kits for most big Japanese bikes of the '70s and '80s. They were imported into the UK by Cobra Road & Racing and Mocheck, both based in London. Though relatively expensive, Martins proved popular.

The space-frame Moto Martin chassis for the Honda CBX1000 was arguably the only successful handling package ever designed for the Honda six-cylinder engine, apart from an Egli. The Moto Martin CBX also looked extremely dramatic; sexy, even.

George Martin left the bike industry in the late '80s, turning to kit car production instead.

The Moto Martin CBX1000 was the best solution to the wayward handling of Honda's six-cylinder flagship.

A Mocheck Martin Kawasaki GPz special of the '80s, captured at the Welsh Motorcycle Show in Builth Wells.

Read Titan

Chris Spedding, the writer of the juke-box classic of the '70s, *Motorbikin'*, rode a Read Titan, fully kitted up, café racer Honda CB250. According to *Superbike* magazine of the early '80s, it featured a 305cc big bore engine, half fairing, clip-ons and even a cigar lighter mounted on the dashboard. In the late '70s, Read Titan also produced a Honda 400/4 special, featuring ARE cast wheels, half fairing, clip-ons and single seat unit, and a futuristic 750 Sabre special.

Read Titan started out in the '60s, and was located near Rivetts leather shop, which meant you could get your bike, and yourself, kitted up in the café racer style in one afternoon in Leytonstone. Handsome.

A Rob North Trident being warmed up in Cadwell's paddock at the classic Beezumph event.

Rob North

A designer in the Triumph race shop of the '60s, Rob North fabricated a frame that helped the BSA/Triumph 750 triples to win races at Daytona, Mallory and many other circuits in the late '60s and early '70s.

Following the collapse of Norton Villiers Triumph in the mid-'70s, North freelanced his frame-making services for those who were still keen on racing British bikes. Piper FM used Rob North frame jigs to design its '70s chassis. A Rob North frame is still regarded as one of the finest starting points for any BSA/Triumph café racer project.

Chris Spedding on his Read Titan Honda in the early '80s.

Rickman

Don and Derek Rickman founded their company in the '50s, and became known as producers of an outstanding MX racing frame. Members of the UK championship motocross team from 1958-68, in 1960 Don was third in the world championship, and British MX champion in '66.

The Rickman frame was a classy piece of Reynolds 531 tubing – nickel-plated, bronze-welded joints and featuring a beautiful bit of bracing around the headstock area. It became known as the Metisse, French for mongrel, but this frame laid the foundations for one of the most successful motorcycle brand names of the '60s and '70s.

Arguably, Rickman stuck with off-road machinery too long, before branching out and housing British and Japanese engines in its road chassis. A special edition Royal Enfield Interceptor was an interesting avenue for Rickman in the late '60s, and the bike made its debut at the Racing and Sporting Show of 1970, complete with footpegs welded directly onto the exhausts and a Lockheed disc brake – pretty advanced for a British bike of the time.

Rickman then moved onto designing chassis kits for bigger Japanese machines. Rickman devised a lightweight, sharp-handling and better braking rolling chassis for the CB750 Honda and Kawasaki Z1 and Z900. These were the flashest Superbikes of the '70s, both of which handled poorly in standard form.

But Rickman could see other opportunites. In 1976, Rickman signed a deal with Honda UK to make fairings and luggage, all branded as Hondastyle in the UK. It also housed Zundapp engines in an off-road frame, and made a small Jeep. Rickman tried hard in the '80s to sell accessories to young British motorcyclists, with the

The Rickman CR rolling chassis kit in 1975 was one of the best ways of utilising the raw power of the big Kawasaki Z1/900 series motors.

Typhoon and Tempest 250cc motorcycle fairings, but the recession of the '80s, plus new learner laws in '82, decimated the UK motorcycle market.

In the mid '80s, Rickman sold the rights to produce the Metisse frame to Pat French, who formed MRD in Bristol. Initial interest was from countries like Japan, and enthusiast demand kept MRD in business into the '90s.

Don and Derek retired to the USA, where they take an interest in classic motorcycles, attending shows and race meetings.

Colin Seeley

A British sidecar racing champion, Colin Seeley is regarded as an accomplished race team manager and innovative frame designer.

As Dave Croxford recalled, Seeley was always meticulous in his approach. "You could eat your dinner from his workshop floor, it was so immaculately clean. He drew lines everywhere, putting every part, or tool in its place. A right fussy bugger."

It was Seeley's early success with a Matchless G50 sidecar racer that taught him valuable lessons about lateral forces and frame flex. He took a Matchless G50 solo race machine in the mid-1960s and designed a frame by hand and eye alone. Seeley knew the importance of precise, tubular frame construction, headstock bracing, and keeping a straight line between headstock and swinging arm pivot.

The MkI and II Seeley-framed bikes won races, with riders like Minter, Hailwood and Blanchard on board. But the real step forward was the MkIII design in the late '60s, when Colin Seeley threw away the duplex cradle idea and drew two rails, directly linking steering head to swinging arm, with the engine suspended from them.

Dave Croxford won the 1968 and 1969 British 500cc championship with the MkIII Seeley G50:

"For me, Colin was perhaps the cleverest bloke this side of Peter Williams – the bikes handled so well you could stuff bigger, faster machinery."

A MkIII Seeley frame was used to house the Norton Commando 750 motor from 1969 onwards, with a road-based version of the bike sold via Gus Kuhn. Barry Sheene rode one of the Seeley-Kuhn Commandos, aged just 19, at Mallory Park in 1970 – his first outing on a big four stroke machine.

Seeley branched out from British bikes, working

This MkIII Seeley G50 was being prepped to appear in the 1998 Assen Centennial in Holland.

with Ducati on the fledgling Imola Ducati 750SS project, the Brabham monocoque racing car chassis, and housing both Suzuki TR500 and QUB two stroke engines in racing frames.

In the mid-'70s, Seeley produced a chassis for the Honda CB750, working with Dixon Racing, which offered a Yoshimura 812cc big bore kit for the Honda 750. The bikes, about 300 in total, were much admired, but when Honda UK decided to produce a Phil Read replica CB750 F2 in 1978, it asked Colin Seeley to leave the frame standard, and essentially 'jazz up' the stock bike. The result was a machine heavier than the standard model.

Seeley also designed 300 limited edition, TL200 trials bikes for Honda, which ended up becoming something of a financial millstone. Following his company's demise, Colin Seeley managed the Crighton-Norton rotary Superbike racing team in the '90s, and remains involved in the classic racing scene to the present day.

Revival

The café racer itself never went away. As a cult object, it remained collectable to the diehard few. But a wider revival within the world of motorcycling started in the early '90s, sparked off by the retro trend.

The Kawasaki Zephyr, Suzuki Bandit and Triumph's Speed Triple 900 all proved there was life in the retro bike format, and there was strong following for the Speed Triple café racer, helped by a one-make racing series in the UK. Interestingly, the Hinckley Speed Triple 900 echoed the one-piece tank/seat/side panel bodywork unit look of the '70s Rickman and Dunstall machines.

Eventually, Hinckley Triumph produced something even closer to its Meriden heritage, in the shape of the Thruxton 900, launched in 2004. Celebrating the '60s Thruxton Bonneville production racer, the modern version featured Ace 'bars, single seat, chequered tape paintwork and was powered by the Bonneville 865cc twin-cylinder motor.

Never slow to see a gap in the market, the Italians picked up on the same retro/café themes in the '90s. The Gilera Saturno 600 was the trailblazer, launched in the late '80s, but it struggled to achieve real sales success.

Speed Triple
Dimensions: Length 2152mm, Width 690mm, Height 1090mm, Seat height 790mm, Wheelbase 1490mm, Weight (dry) 209kg. Fuel capacity: 25 litres. Colours: Fireball Orange, Diablo Black.

Engine and Transmission. Triumph's classic liquid-cooled, DOHC Triple in café racer form. With a bore and stroke of 76 x 65mm and a compression ratio of 10.6:1, triple 36mm flat slide CV carburettors and digital inductive electronic ignition, this muscle delivers nearly a hundred horses - 98PS at 9,000rpm and 83Nm of torque at 6,500rpm. Driving through a wet multiplate clutch and a 5-speed gearbox, and weighing in at just 209kg, it is quick and responsive. The rev limiter cuts in at 9,700rpm. **Frame and Suspension.** Strength comes from a micro alloyed high tensile steel frame with an aluminium alloy swinging arm incorporating an eccentric chain adjuster. Whatever your riding style you can adjust the suspension to suit. The 43mm front forks, which feature triple rate springs, and the rear monoshock are both adjustable for preload and rebound damping. The front forks are also adjustable for compression damping.

Brakes and Wheels. Stopping power is taken care of by two 310mm floating discs and two 4 piston calipers up front and one 255mm disc and 2 piston caliper at the rear, with a frame mounted torque arm.

Wheels are black 3-spoke alloys, 17" x 3.5" on the front fitted with a 120/70 ZR17 and to help you hang onto the rear, a 17" x 5.5" rim with meaty 180/55 ZR17 rubber.

Seat cowl shown on the Speed Triple is an extra cost accessory item available from authorised Triumph dealers.

The original Speed Triple 900 of the '90s is a cult bike now.

The Triumph Thruxton 900, pictured in 2005 colours.

Moto Guzzi offered tuned versions of its 1100 Sport, the RS and the Corsa, and Guzzi put the Le Mans badge onto its V11 roadster, but the bike lacked the low slung, elegant beauty of the original '70s Le Mans.

Rival Ducati waited until the 21st century before launching its Sport Classic series, with a stripped-down 1000S, plus a limited edition Paul Smart replica. They looked good, but lacked an edge somehow. It took specialists to make Italian café racers with true pizazz, like Baines Racing, which put together a stunning Imola '72 replica, whilst Bimota produced the gorgeous DB5R in 2007, essentially a homage to its own DB series bikes from the '80s.

The Gilera Saturno was a return to the single-cylinder race rep format of the '50s and '60s.

The Suzuki Goose was an oddball homage to the original 350 British café racers of the '50s.

BSA Regal in Southampton produced the Gold SR500, a natty blend of Yamaha single-cylinder power and its own chassis.

Motorcycling's roots, made retro

Other manufacturers took the less hi-tech road in the '90s, using the old Gold Star, Velocette Venom or Norton Dominator as their inspiration.

Suzuki's quirky Goose 350, BSA Regal's retro SR500 and Honda's clubman-style GB500 TT all ploughed the retro furrow, being essentially modern interpretations of the old single-cylinder sporty models of the '50s.

The BSA Regal SR500 had a cradle frame, drum brake and genuine retro style. It was a success in Japan, where the mix of punchy Yamaha XT500 dirt bike motor and British-designed chassis offered a realistic taste of the past, but without the unreliability or feeble brakes of '50s technology.

Yamaha itself saw scope in the café racer format and in 1996 launched the Italian-designed SZR660 and the twin-cylinder, trellis-framed TRX850. But although the TRX – or Trixie as it was nicknamed – attracted some fans, with Dutch chassis specialist Nico Bakker making a one-off special based around the 850 parallel twin, Yamaha quietly dropped both models after a few years.

Kawasaki meanwhile paid homage to the BSA A10 with its W650 twin in the late '90s. Tuning and accessory shops in Germany and Japan still cater for this cult bike today, and Rickman-framed versions have been created by devoted fans. Despite some success, the W650 was dropped from Kawasaki's European range in 2003.

If there was real revival in interest in all things traditional, and café racer, where did the manufacturers go wrong?

Perhaps the root of the problem is that a true café racer remains a machine created by enthusiasts,

The TRX850 of the '90s was sold as a Japanese Ducati, but it didn't quite have the kudos of the Italian brand.

individuals, not corporate marketing teams. The café racer phenomenon came from back street sheds, race circuits and workshops. Dave Degens, Ian Kennedy and Paul Dunstall all started making their bikes for the sport, the fun of improving on what was coming out of the factories.

The café racer was always a special, a one-off. When the manufacturers make thousands of them, it kind of dilutes the magic.

Steve Elliot's tribute to Wayne Gardner captured the spirit of the early '80s superbike/production race series in Europe and the USA.

Time travellers

As the '90s progressed, older riders started to either restore classic café racers, or create their own proddie racer machines. Cumbrian Steve Elliot built a Wayne Gardner, '80s Moriwaki replica in the mid-1990s.

"Wayne was a hero of mine," Steve told *Northern Biker* magazine back in 1995, "and I wanted a road bike just like his early '80s proddie racer. Something that had a big-bore Kawasaki engine, modified Z1R frame and details like Lockheed brakes, Barnett clutch, no side panels and so on. It took me eight years to build and I went through three girlfriends, which says something about me ... but I'm not sure what."

Elliot's Moriwaki was a celebration of a particular era of Japanese motorcycle production racing, when wild streetbikes were tamed by riders like Freddie Spencer, Gardner and Lawson. Elliot was searching for the roots of his biking addiction, the machine you once had as a poster on your bedroom wall.

It was the same affection for the glory days of British racing that kept specialist bike builders in the game through the lean years of the '80s and '90s.

"We started making the Hyde Harrier in 1987," recalled Norman Hyde, "as a road version of the old '70s Triumph Trident proddie racer. The Hyde Harrier was a chance to imagine how the Trident T160 and Bonneville T140 might have developed, if they'd been housed in a Harris chassis, used modern brakes, wheels, lights, etc., and then raced."

The '80s and '90s Hyde Harrier chassis kits featured a spartan tubular frame designed by Steve

Les Williams produced the Buccaneer in the '80s, pictured here next to a Harley-Davidson-powered café racer.

The revived Hyde Harrier uses a tuned Hinckley Bonneville twin-cylinder motor, optional Ohlins suspension, and a Harris frame.

and Lester Harris, who had worked with GP race teams and developed their famous 'Magnum' frames for streetfighter bikes. Modern Harrier touches included Astralite cast wheels, Marzocchi forks, Lockheed disc brakes and twin Koni shocks.

"The Harrier was a success," recalled Norman, "especially when I re-launched it at the NEC Motorcycle Show in the late '80s, by employing a pretty girl to walk around the stand completely naked. Amazing how that got more coverage than anything else at the show that year!"

Fast forward to the 21st century and Norman Hyde is now making an all-new Harrier chassis kit available for the Hinckley 865cc Bonneville twin.

"I thought that Triumph probably wouldn't do a full-on, café racer version of the modern Bonneville," observed Norman, "so the 50th anniversary seemed the perfect time to do another Harrier. Pick the best chassis for the Hinckley Bonneville engine, which is much the same ethos as others applied with the original Tritons."

Meanwhile UK importers of Indian-made Enfield Bullet bikes had a more modest ambition.

Phil Turner from *Motorcycle Sport & Leisure* magazine takes the café racer-styled Enfield clubman for a refreshing spin.

"We wanted to create a retro single-cylinder café racer, something inspired by the old Coninental GT," commented Peter Rivers-Fletcher at Watosnian-Squire. "We took the basic 500 Bullet and added our own exhaust, bigger carb and the traditional single seat, clip-ons and long alloy fuel tank."

Re-engineering the past

Motorcycles get in the blood, and it's often the case that a lifelong passion for speed and all things two-wheeled is passed from father to son. Café racer builder Steve Carpenter was born and raised in London, into a family of motorcycle enthusiasts.

"My Dad told me stories about how he and mates raced from London to the Busy Bee at Watford, or to a café in Birmingham back in the '40s. He built a Brough Superior special to try and win. All of them were dicing flat out, with no helmets, just work clothes on. Talk about finding out who had the biggest balls!"

Steve in the '90s, fettling his Bonneville.

One of Steve Carpenter's modern interpretations of the Honda CR750 from the early '70s.

Steve spent the '80s despatch riding in London, and once delivered a package to Princess Margaret, who was surprisingly laid-back for a member of the Royal Family:

"I dropped off the parcel, she signed for it with a fag going in her mouth, then I rooster-tailed the bike down the driveway. She just smiled at me, classy old bird." says Steve.

In the '90s, Steve emigrated, first to Australia, then the USA. He spotted a gap in the market for retro Japanese café racers.

"I have rock stars, regular joes, all kinds of guys buying my café-style CB750s," said Steve Carpenter, "and it all got going because I got some web TV thing back in 2000. It just took off, it was like people were fed up with bland modern stuff. They wanted something from an era when bikes were still kinda dangerous."

The modern day Tritons produced by Dave Degens and Unity Equipe, or the sleek Norvil Commandos, demonstrate an enduring passion for big, beefy British bikes. The Norvil Motorcycle Company in Staffordshire has been building replica Norton Commandos since the '80s, and began to make Norton 650SS café racers and a production racer 850 early in the 21st century.

"We're re-manufacturing a great British bike, and imagining how it might have changed in the '80s and '90s," said Kate Emery, daughter of Norvil's founder Les Emery. "There are riders all over the world who want a modern-day Commando, so we add 12 or 14 inch disc brakes, halogen lights, electronic ignition and some improvements to the Isolastic engine mounts. It's all about making the bike more practical to ride, a better performer all round – but making sure it still looks and sounds like a proper motorbike."

Jackie at Unity Equipe, makers of Tritons since the late 1950s, agrees that sympathetically updating the fabulous machines of the past is the way ahead.

The Norvil Norton 650SS café racer, a fusion of modern electrics, uprated brakes and the traditional appeal of the Dominator twins from the '60s.

The Norvil Production racer is a tribute to the race-winning Commando of the '70s, but available with modern technology which makes it a safe, yet fast machine.

"It is getting harder to have one-off parts made in the UK," said Jackie, "but we're determined to keep the essence of what John Tickle was doing at Unity back in the '60s. We still make the Manx Nortons and the Tritons along the same design lines, but we're starting to offer a Triton chassis that can take the Hinckley twins and triples. It's capturing the spirit of the past that counts."

The Rocker scene never went away entirely in the '80s and '90s. Len Patterson began a series of Rockers' reunions with runs to Brighton, and helped organise '50s 'rock 'n' roll' gigs at Battersea Town Hall.

"They were piss-ups basically, but great fun," recalled Lenny, who was a regular visitor to the '59 Club and Chelsea Bridge in the '60s and '70s.

The Ace Café re-opens

In 1994 Mark Wilsmore staged an Ace Café Reunion to mark the 25th anniversary of it closing, and to celebrate the heritage of the original Ace.

"From the moment I put that out to the clubs and motorcycle press, my phone rang 24/7," recalled Mark. "Within a couple of weeks, I had two sacks of mail at the PO Box number I'd set up – the interest was incredible, and worldwide."

The '94 Ace Café Reunion attracted some 12,000 bikes, and Mark considered repeating the event in '95 at Brighton. Those plans never quite worked out, so a back-up venue at London's Chelsea Bridge was arranged and another healthy turnout showed the huge level of support for the idea of the original Ace becoming a riders meeting place once again.

Over the next few years Mark completed the buy-out of the tyre-fitting business that occupied the Ace Café

Pete Fischer meets café racer fans at Chelsea Bridge in 1995.

Café racer fans from Germany ride over to the Ace on their modified W650s – Kawasaki's modern take on the BSA A10 twin.

The Rockers never went away, and the Chelsea Bridge saw a reunion in 1995, before the Ace Café re-opened in 1997.

premises. In December 1997, the Ace Café re-opened for business, selling tea, bacon sandwiches and offering London's café racers a warm welcome home.

"That was a fantastic day," recalls Wilsmore, "and I saw grown men with tears in their eyes as they walked through those famous doors once again, hearing Eddie Cochran on the juke-box and seeing a line of Triumphs, Nortons and BSAs parked up outside.

"Since then we've had almost every type of car and bike night you can imagine, had TV shows and documentaries made here, books written at the Ace, bike shows, and attracted over 100,000 people to the Brighton Reunion every September.

"People come from Japan, Australia, Scandanavia ... all over the world, just to have a mug of tea at the Ace. It's the Graceland of café racer culture, a slice of biking heaven."

Jurgen Hartel at Brighton in September 2006.

Neil Harrison rode from Lancashire to Brighton in September 2006.

Ace faces

The Ace Café today plays host to many events, but the Brighton Burn-Up each September is regarded as one of the best weekends, attracting tens of thousands from the UK and many more from mainland Europe, Japan, the USA, Australia, etc.

Jurgen Hartel from Germany attended in 2006 on his Kawasaki W650 café racer:

"I have a BSA Gold Star as well, which I suppose many people would say is the real thing, whereas the W650 is an imitation café racer. But the Goldie is just for Sundays, the W650 is something that you can use to travel hundreds of miles on.

I rode over here on the Kawasaki from Munich with my buddies, great fun. For me, the Ace Café captures the real spirit of the '50s and '60s; the bikes, the music, the rebellion – it's everything that made riding a bike cool."

Another rider, Neil Harrison from Lancashire, was on his BSA Spitfire 650, and explained why he still sports a quiff and leather jacket, even in his mid-forties. "It's about getting back to a time when motorcycling was more pure somehow," said Neil. "Bikes back in the '60s were more honest, so were the riders. It was everyday transport and people had to learn to fix them, you got your hands dirty.

Marta, also known as Little Miss Dynamite.

Marta dancing to a soundtrack of '50s rock 'n' roll.

"I think nowadays some riders have a particular machine as some type of fashion statement, but that's not for me. I love the rock 'n' roll era, the cafés, the bikes. Why live in misery-arse modern Britain when the '50s were a much simpler, probably happier time?"

One of the real characters at the 2006 Brighton Burn-Up was Marta. The author first noticed her jiving in the car park at the Ace.

"I have an AJS model 16," said Marta, originally from Barcelona, but then living in London, "and I would love a fast Triton, or a Norton. What's not to like about

these old motorcycles, and the Ace Café? The clothes, the music, the speed. The whole thing is a little bit naughty and I love that. I would live next door to the Ace if I could, it's the best place to be."

Tragically, Marta died on the Brighton Burn-Up in 2007, but her fiery spirit lives on in the shape of the Ace Café 'Little Miss Dynamite' café racer motorbike, created by Nick Gale at the Stonebridge Motorcycle Company. The bike features a potent S&S V-twin engine, the classic long fuel tank, single seat and loud, upswept exhaust pipes. Marta would approve.

The future

The café racer motorcycle lives on, but it is better as a fond memory, rather than a concept for blending the very best modern components? Paul Dunstall thinks modern machines are so good, there's no way you can make a modern version of the Triton.

"Modern 600s make what, 130bhp? How can you significantly tune an engine like that, and why would you need to? But more to he point, I don't see how you could make your own bike now and win a Superbike race against factory opposition. Big teams, big budgets, hi-tech – it's all different."

Jackie at Unity Equipe sees the future as being a remix of the past, with the accent on reliability of modern engines and electrical systems: "The Hinckley Triumph engines, like the Bonnie and the Thruxton twins, are the future for us. A Unity bike will hopefully remain a true British bike, something that has the style of a '60s Triton, but is easy to service, more fun to own."

Then again, collectors are tracking down some of the great café racers of the past and restoring them, or updating them. Will Mellor from Cheshire found an S&S Saxon Turbo, featuring a Rickman chassis, once used on stage by the rock band Saxon.

"There were only ten made, and this one was used on stage, clocked up a few hundred miles in the '70s and '80s before being stored and forgotten. I stripped it completely, took the GSXR1100 back end off it, recalibrated the turbo boost gauge – it was reading 5psi when it had 15psi running in there – and had the bike re-painted. It was two years work, but what a feeling riding it on the road."

The S&S Saxon Turbo has won awards at various shows alongside Tritons, Norvins and many more. Café racers are now being recognised by classic

Turbo-charged Kawasaki motor, Rickman chassis. The rock band Saxon knew how to raise some hell back in the '70s.

Garish maybe, but this Dresda Honda 900 from 1980 is definitely one of a kind.

enthusiasts as being just as worthy of restoration to concours condition as a Vincent Black Lightning or a Kawasaki Z1.

Eamon Maloney has been a fan of Japanese café racers since the late '70s and sees the classic scene changing: "Nowadays it's getting hard to restore a Japanese machine to original condition, as eBay has driven parts prices through the roof. I think a lot of guys who rode Japanese bikes from the '70s to the '90s will create their own café racers from older, less expensive bikes, because you cannot go the concours route now without spending a fortune."

Eamon is a big fan of '70s café racers and owns Rickman, Seeley and Dresda Honda specials. The Dresda was built by Dave Degens for an *MCN* 'Mark the Moto-Ball' competition back in the late '70s, with an over-the-top paint job by Leon Wallace.

"I like the Rickman, the frame is beautiful, but some of the panels, the brackets, and so on, suggest that it was built to a price in a factory," said Eamon. "The Dresda is more individual, it's a pure, one-off piece of motorcycle engineering and, whether you like it or not, that's what I admire about the whole café racer phenomenon. It's ultimately about standing out from the crowd."

Parts & services directory

This is not a comprehensive, global listing of every company active in the café racer restoration, servicing, spares or complete bike building business. It is as accurate and detailed as humanly possible, and correct at the time of going to print.

We hope you find it useful in keeping your café racer, or classic motorcycle on the road, or in creating your own dream bike.

Please note, we have mainly used UK-based distributor, manufacturer or dealer details. If you are looking for spares, you will find specialist parts suppliers listed by motorcycle marque.

Ace 'bars
Disco Volante, Anglesey, Wales
Tel: 01490 412 621
www.discovolantemoto.com
Range of ace-bars and clip-ons.

AJS
AJS Motorcycles, Andover, Hampshire, England
Tel: 01264 710 074
www.ajs-shop.co.uk
AJS off-road classic spare parts.

AJS Matchless Owners Club, Kettering, Northamptonshire, England
Tel: 01536 511 532
www.jampot.com
Technical helpline for members, spares, advice, rallies etc.

AMC Classic Spares
Tel: 01462 811 770
www.amcclassicspares.com
Large stock of AJS and Matchless spares.

Alternators
West Country Windings, Plymouth, Devon, England
Tel: 01752 560 906
New or exchange alternators, mail order service.

Ariel
Draganfly Motorcycles, Bungay, Suffolk, England
Tel: 01986 894 798
www.draganfly.co.uk
Ariel spares, accessories and gifts.

BMW
BMW Motorworks
Tel: 0845 458 0077
www.motorworks.com
Large supplier of new and used BMW parts.

Moto-Bins, Spalding, Lincolnshire, England
Tel: 01775 680 881
www.motobins.co.uk
BMW spares, distributor of Hepco and Becker.

Bodywork
Jap4 Performance, Greater Manchester, England
Tel: 0161 613 6600
www.jap4performance.com
Supplier of Tyga and Silhouette body parts, fairings, etc.

Mead Speed, Milton Keynes, Buckinghamshire, England
Tel: 01908 610 311

www.meadspeed.com
Wide range for café racers – fuel tanks, mudguards, fairings, screens and more.

Brakes

AJS Motorcycles, Andover, Hampshire, England
Tel: 01264 710 074
www.ajs-shop.co.uk
Grimeca drum brakes and spare parts.

Goodridge UK
Tel: 01392 369 090
www.goodridge.net
Decades of experience in road and racing brake hoses, fittings, etc.

Andy Molnar Manx Norton, Lancashire, England
Tel: 01772 700 700
www.manx.co.uk
Replica Fontana drum brakes.

Saftek, Cleckheaton, West Yorkshire, England
Tel: 01274 862 666
www.saftek.co.uk
Brake shoes relined, alloy brake shoe castings, all makes, models, etc.

BSA

C&D Autos, Henley-in-Arden, Warwickshire, England
Tel: 01564 795 000
Wide range of BSA parts available.

Cake Street Classics, Woodbridge, Suffolk, England
Tel: 01986 798 504
BSA A7/A10 specialist, new and secondhand parts.

Pete Hammond Motorcycles, Cirencester, Gloucestershire, England
Tel: 01285 640 098
www.hammondmotorcycles.co.uk
Wide range of BSA parts, 1958 onwards.

Hawkshaw Motorcycles, Merseyside, England
Tel: 0151 931 4488
www.hawkshawmotorcycles.com
Wide range of BSA spares 1950s onwards.

George Prew
Tel: 01763 848 763
BSA Gold Star and A10 specialist.

RJM Classics, Arlesey, Bedfordshire, England
Tel: 01462 835 970
www.rjmclassic.com
BSA, Enfield and Triumph specialist, service and repair.

SRM Engineering
Tel: 01970 627 771
www.srm-engineering.com
BSA parts and rebuilds, recon gearboxes built, spares and parts manufactured, plus restoration service.

Spitfire Products, Knutsford, Cheshire, England
Tel: 01565 632 991

BSA spares and advice from the '50s models onwards, Small Heath factory experience.

Steve Tonkin Restorations, Ulverston, Lancashire, England
Tel: 01524 825 205
BSA Gold Star specialist – cranks, clutches, 5 speed gearboxes.

Cables

Brit Bits, Christchurch, Dorset, England
Tel: 01202 483 675
www.motorcycle-uk.com
Wide range of control cables for most classic British bikes.

Carrot Cycles, Fiskerton, Lincolnshire, England
Tel: 01522 595 975
www.carrotcycles.co.uk
Control cables made to order.

Café race builders

Baines Racing, Silverstone, Northamptonshire, England
Tel: 01327 858 510
www.bainesracing.co.uk
Ducati 750SS Imola replicas built using modern Ducati base machines.

CB750café.com, California, USA
www.cb750café.com
Steve Carpenter specialises in Honda CB750 '70s-style café racers.

Dresda Autos, Rusper, West Sussex, England
Tel: 01293 871 887
www.dresda.co.uk
Still run by Dave Degens, original Triton specialist.

Hogbitz, Chigwell, Essex, England
Tel: 020 8500 9025
www.hogbitz.com
Builders of Harley engined café racers to your spec.

Norman Hyde, Rugby, Warwickshire, England
Tel: 01926 497 375
www.normanhyde.co.uk
Meriden and Hinckley Triumph café racer specialist, with tuning, engine parts, big bore kits and rolling chassis kits all available. Builder of the Harrier.

JMC Classics, Royston, Hertfordshire, England
Tel: 01763 249 600
www.jmcclassics.com
Builders of new Egli Vincents in the UK, restorations undertaken.

Andy Molnar Manx Norton, Lancashire, England
Tel: 01772 700 700
www.manx.co.uk
Builder of Manx Norton, AJS 7R G5 replicas. Fontana drum brake replicas.

Norvil Motorcycle Co., Burntwood, Staffordshire, England
Tel: 01543 278 008
www.norvilmotorcycle.co.uk
Norton Commando production racer/café racers built to your spec.

The Stonebridge Motorcycle Company, 250 Water Road, Wembley, Middlesex, England
Tel: 020 8998 6775
www.stonebridgemotorcompany.com
Builder of the Ace Café/Little Miss Dynamite machine.

Unity Equipe, Todmorden, Lancashire, England
Tel: 01706 839 059
www.unityequipe.com
Triton, Triumph and Manx Norton builder, spares, accessories.

Watsonian-Squire, Blockley, Gloucestershire, England
Tel: 01386 700 907
www.watsonian-squire.com
Importer of Enfield Indian Bullet, manufacturer of the Enfield Bullet Clubman 500 (UK only) café racer variant.

Carburettors

Allens Performance
Tel: 01949 836 733
www.allensperformance.co.uk
UK importer for Keihin and Mikuni carbs.

Amal Carb Company, Salisbury, Wiltshire, England
Tel: 01722 412 500
Email: info@amalcarb.co.uk
Amal carburettors and fitting kits.

Euro Carb Ltd
Tel: 0118 943 1180
www.dellorto.co.uk
UK Dell Orto carb distributor since 1968.

Surrey Cycles, Cranleigh, Surrey, England
Tel: 01483 272 328
Amal carb specialist supplier.

Chassis kits

Norman Hyde, Rugby, Warwickshire, England
Tel: 01926 497 375
www.normanhyde.co.uk
Meriden and Hinckley Triumph café racer specialist, with tuning, engine parts, big bore kits and rolling chassis kits all available.

Rickman, Fowlers of Bristol, England
Tel: 01179 719 200.
Advice on Rickman products, some spares.

Unity Equipe, Rochdale, Lancashire, England
Tel: 01706 839 059
www.unityequipe.com
Triton and Manx replica builders, spares or complete bikes.

Chrome plating

CCB, Carshalton, Surrey, England
Tel: 020 8647 3123
www.collinschemicalblacking.co.uk
Blasting, polishing, nickel and chrome plating, etc.

Cumbria Plating Services, Carlisle, Cumbria, England
Tel: 01228 819 324
Chrome, copper, gold, zinc and nickel plating.

Niphos Metal Finishing Co., Hope Street, Crewe, Cheshire, England
Tel: 01270 214 081
Chrome, nickel and copper plating, general metal polishing.

Clothing

Lewis Leathers, London, England
Tel: 020 7402 0863
www.lewisleathers.com
Classic leather jackets, boots and other clothing in a traditional style.

Moto Central, Nuneaton, Warwickshire, England
Tel: 024 7634 7870
www.motocentral.co.uk
Ruby helmets, Belstaff clothing.

Silvermans, Mile End, London, England
Tel: 020 77900 900
www.silvermans.co.uk
Classic leather jackets; Belstaff, Vanson, etc. Boots, Davida helmets.

Sunstuff Quality Clothing
www.sunstuffclassics.com
Classic all-season riding kit.

Crankshafts

Nourish Racing Engine Co, Oakham, Leicestershire, England
Tel: 01572 722 712
Crankshafts machined from billet, balanced, etc. Valve kits, con-rods, etc.

Service Exchange Parts, Kegworth, Derby
Tel: 01509 673 295
Crankshafts re-built, all engine work undertaken.

Cylinder heads

The Cylinder Head Shop, Wormley, Surrey, England
Tel: 01428 685 883
www.cylinderheadshop.co.uk
Serdi equipped head centre, all makes, all models catered for.

Ducati

Mdina Italia
Tel: 0845 680 9005
Email: mdinaitalia@googlemail.com
Conti silencers supplied, plus a range of Italian bike spares.

Electrics

Boyer Bransden, Maidstone, Kent, England
Tel: 01622 730 930
www.boyerbransden.com
Manufacturer of electronic ignitions for wide range of motorcycles, classic and modern. Denso spark plug stockist.

Dave Lindsley, Heywood, Lancashire, England
Tel: 01706 365 838
www.davelindsley.co.uk
Magneto and dynamo repair, plus on-line spares catalogue.

Motorcycle Electrical Services, Warwick, Warwickshire, England
Tel: 01926 499 756
www.motorcycle-electrical.co.uk
Manufacture and design of wiring harness for most British classics.

Enfield

Watsonian-Squire, Blockley, Gloucestershire, England
Tel: 01386 700 907
www.watsonian-squire.com

Importer of Enfield India machines in the UK, spares, tuning and service advice.

Engine servicing
Wheeltons, WGW, Chorley, Lancashire, England
Tel: 01254 832 008
Specialist service and repair of classic British and Japanese bikes.

Engine works/tuning
B & Y Engineering, Somerton, Somerset, England
Tel: 01458 270 004
Email: info@byengineering.co.uk
Engine rebuilds, road or race tuning, blasting, welding, etc.

Norman Hyde, Rugby, Warwickshire, England
Tel: 01926 497 375
www.normanhyde.co.uk
Meriden and Hinckley Triumph specialist, with tuning, engine parts, big bore kits and advice all available.

Nourish Racing Engine Co., Oakham, Leicestershire, England
Tel: 01572 722 712
Crankshafts machined from billet, balanced, etc. Valve kits, con-rods, etc.

Service Exchange Parts, Kegworth, Derby, England
Tel: 01509 673 295
Crankshafts rebuilt, all engine work undertaken.

Exhausts
Armours Ltd, Bournemouth, Dorset, England
Tel: 01202 519 409

www.armoursltd.co.uk
Wide range of exhausts for most classic bikes.

Mdina Italia
Tel: 0845 680 9005
Email: mdinaitalia@googlemail.com
Conti silencers supplied, plus a range of Italian bike spares.

Fairings & footrests
Disco Volante, Anglesey, Wales
Tel: 01490 412 621
www.discovolantemoto.com
Range of glass-fibre fairings, bodywork, footrests and bike controls for many classic bikes.

Frames
Harris Performance, Hertford, Hertfordshire, England
Tel: 01992 532501
www.harris-performance.com
Road and race frame design and fabrication

Fuel tanks
Merlin Classic Motorcycles, Atherstone, Warwickshire, England
Tel: 01827 874 572
Flexible fuel tank sealant kits, repairs to tanks.

The Tank Shop
Tel: 01387 740 259
www.thetankshop.com
Wide range of alloy café racer tanks.

Wassell Ltd
Tel: 01522 888 444

www.totalbikebits.com
Wide range of British bike spares, including fuel tanks for BSA, Norton, Matchless, etc.

Gearboxes

Quaife Engineering, Sevenoaks, Kent, England
Tel: 01732 741 144
One-off gearbox design and production, from modern competition transmissions to classic Norton five- and six-speed gearboxes. Service and rebuilds undertaken.

Gloves

Chequered Flag, Prenton, Merseyside, England
Tel: 0151 652 4241
www.chequeredflag.com
Traditional gauntlet-style gloves supplied, plus modern designs.

Helmets

Davida, Birkenhead, Merseyside, England
Tel: 0151 647 2419
www.davida.co.uk
UK's last manufacturer of motorcycle helmets, all hand-made, leather linings, custom paintwork.

Moto Central, Nuneaton, Warwickshire, England
Tel: 024 7634 7870
www.exclusivehelmets.com
Importers for Ruby open face helmets in the UK.

Honda

David Silver Spares, Leiston, Suffolk, England
Tel: 01728 833 020
www.davidsilverspares.com
Huge range of Honda spares, online ordering facility.

Tippetts Motors, London, England
Tel: 020 8399 2417
www.honda-tippetts.co.uk
Honda spares from the '60s onwards.

Insurance

Carole Nash Insurance Consultants, Altrincham, Cheshire, England
Tel: 0800 093 5599
www.carolenash.com
Classic motorcycles, specials and modern machines all insured. Agreed values, multibike policies, off-road cover, helmet and leathers, personal injury, etc.

Footman James
Tel: 0845 458 6737
www.footmanjames.co.uk
Classic and vintage bikes insured, personal accident cover, legal expenses, multi-bike policies.

Lynbrook Insurance
Tel: 0845 130 4662
Classic insurance on bikes 15 years or older, salvage buy-back option, laid-up cover, agreed mileage limits, etc.

Peter Best
Tel: 01376 573 033
www.classicinsurance.co.uk
All classic and modern motorcycles insured, home and contents cover.

Instruments

L P Williams, Claughton, Lancashire, England
Tel: 01524 770 956

Replica Smiths speedo and tacho for Triumphs, Trident T150/160 specialist.

Speedo Repairs, Frimley Green, Surrey, England
Tel: 01252 835 353
www.speedorepairs.co.uk
British bike clocks specialist, 12 month guarantee.

Kawasaki

Classic Kawasaki Club
www.classickawasaki.com
Kawasaki triples specialist club.

Straightline Racing, Suffolk, England
Tel: 01553 772 774
Air-cooled Kawasaki fours specialist, tuning, spares, rebuilds.

Z1 Enterprise Inc., USA
Tel: 001 315 926 5054
www.z1enterprises.com
Kawasaki Z1 specialist, wide range of spares for Kawasaki air-cooled fours, Z1 replica parts.

Z Power, Leigh, Lancashire, England
Tel: 01942 262 864
www.z-power.co.uk
Kawasaki Z1, air-cooled fours and two-stroke models specialist.

Laverda

Slater Laverda
Tel: 01885 410 295
www.slaterlaverda.com
Laverda specialist since 1970, spares and advice.

Matchless

AJS Matchless Owners Club, Kettering, Northamptonshire, England
Tel: 01536 511 532
www.jampot.com
Technical helpline for members, spares, advice, rallies, etc.

AMC Classic Spares
Tel: 01462 811 770
www.amcclassicspares.com
Large stock of AJS and Matchless spares.

Mirrors

Halcyon Classic Parts, Ware, Hertfordshire, England
Tel: 01920 486 032
www.classicpartsltd.com
Bar-end mirrors in various styles.

Moto Guzzi

Corsa Italiana, Colliers Wood, London, England
Tel: 020 8540 7155
www.corsaitaliana.com.
Guzzi spares from 1968 onwards.

Mdina Italia
Tel: 0845 680 9005.
Email: mdinaitalia@googlemail.com
Conti silencers supplied, plus a range of Italian bike spares.

Motori di Marino, Chiltington, Surrey, England
Tel: 01798 813 260
Moto Guzzi specialist spares, service and advice.

Norton

Hawkshaw Motorcycles,
Merseyside, England
Tel: 0151 931 4488
www.hawkshawmotorcycles.com
Wide range of Norton spares 1950s
onwards.

Mick Hemmings Motorcycles
Tel: 01604 638 505
Six speed gearboxes, spares, tuning, all things Norton.

Norton Owners Club, Lower Bullingham, Herefordshire, England
www.nortonownersclub.org
Roadholder magazine, advice, shows, runs and events.

Norvil Motorcycle Co., Burntwood, Staffordshire, England
Tel: 01543 278 008
Norton Dominator and Commando specialist, rebuilds, brake upgrades, spares and advice.

RGM Motors, Beckermet, Cumbria, England
Tel: 01946 841 517
Norton specialists, spares, Manx-style fuel tanks, exhausts.

SRM Engineering
Tel: 01970 627 771
www.srm-engineering.com
Norton parts and rebuilds, recon gearboxes built, spares and parts manufactured, plus restoration service.

Nuts and bolts

Custom Fasteners Ltd., Newtown, Powys, Wales

Tel: 01686 629 666
www.custom-fasteners.co.uk
Chrome, stainless nuts and bolts.

Oil tanks

Mead Speed, Milton Keynes, Buckinghamshire, England
Tel: 01908 610 311
www.meadspeed.com
Central alloy oil tanks for café racers, fuel tanks, fairings, screens and more.

Oils

Castrol Classic Oils
Tel: 01954 231 668
Extensive range of lubricants for classic motorcycles.

Morris Lubricants, Shrewsbury, Shropshire, England
Tel: 01743 232 200.
Email: info@morris-lubricants.co.uk
Wide range of lubricants for classic and modern machines.

Paint

The Finishing Touch, Chelmsford, Essex, England
Tel: 01245 400 918
Parts repaired and painted, free estimates.

Priest Motor Bodies, Altrincham, Cheshire, England
Tel: 0161 928 3210
Fuel tank and tinware repairs, show-winning paintwork.

RS Bike Paint, Welham Green, Hertfordshire, England
Tel: 01707 273 219
www.rsbikepaint.co.uk
Mail order service, touch-ups motorcycle specialists.

Polishing

CCB, Carshalton, Surrey, England
Tel: 020 8647 3123
www.collinschemicalblacking.co.uk
Blasting, polishing, nickel and chrome plating, etc.

Perfect Polishing Atherstone, Warwickshire, England
Tel: 01827 717 606
www.perfectpolishingkits.co.uk
General polishing kits, grinding machines.

Powder coating

Elite Engineering, Aintree, Merseyside, England
Tel: 0151 524 2838
Powder coating, blasting, alloy and stainless welding.

Foremost Coatings, Felbridge, Surrey, England
Tel: 01342 833 455
Powder coating, bead and grit blasting.

Goldburn Finishers, Bordon, Hampshire, England
Tel: 01420 477 696
www.goldburnfinishers.co.uk

Microblast, Windsor, Berkshire, England
Tel: 01753 620 145
Frames and swingarms shot blasted, powder-coated.

Triple S Powder Coating, Bingley, Yorkshire, England
Tel: 01274 562 474
www.Triple-S.co.uk
Motorcycle coating specialist.

Restoration

Hailwood Motocycle Restorations Ltd., Buntingford, Hertfordshire, England
Tel: 01763 271 444
www.hailwoodrestorations.com
All types of motorcycles restored, service and repair.

George Hopwood, Sidcup, Kent, England
Tel: 020 8300 9573
Triumph Thruxton specialist, T100, T120 models.

Robin James Engineering Services, Leominster, Herefordshire, England
Tel: 01568 612 800
www.robinjamesengineering.com
All classic motorcycles restored and cared for.

Jeca Motorcycle Restoration
Tel: 01621 772 074
Email: jnfjeca@btconnect.com
Restoration from a box of bits to show-winning standard.

Royal Enfield

Charnwood Classic Restorations. Coalville, Leicestershire, England
Tel: 01530 832 634
www.charnwoodclassic.com
Sidecar specialists and Royal Enfield Bullet specialist.

Watsonian-Squire, Blockley, Gloucestershire, England
Tel: 01386 700 907
www.watsonian-squire.com
Importer of Enfield India machines, spares, technical advice, etc.

Seats

Bagster, St Asaph, Denbighshire, Wales
Tel: 01745 823 333
www.bagster.com
Design your own one-off seat, seat covers.

David Silver Spares, Leiston, Suffolk, England
Tel: 01728 833 020
www.davidsilverspares.com
Huge range of seats for Hondas, online ordering facility.

R K Leighton, Birmingham, West Midlands, England
Tel: 0121 359 0514
www.rk-leighton.co.uk
New and rebuilt seats for most classic British bikes.

Sidecars

Charnwood Classic Restorations, Coalville, Leicestershire, England
Tel: 01530 832 634
www.charnwoodclassic.com
Sidecar specialist and Royal Enfield Bullet specialist.

Watsonian-Squire, Blockley, Gloucestershire, England
Tel: 01386 700 907
www.watsonian-squire.com
The world's longest established sidecar maker, all classic and modern machines catered for, plus trailers manufactured. UK importers of Enfield India machines.

Spares

Please search by machine make.

Suspension

FitForx Fork Repairs, London, England
www.fitforx.co.uk
General fork repairs, renovation, coating, etc.

Hagon Products Ltd., Hainault, Essex, England
Tel: 0208 502 6222
www.hagon-shocks.co.uk
Manufacturer of classic shock absorbers, one-off designs, seat-lowering shock kits.

Jap4 Performance, Greater Manchester, England
Tel: 0161 613 6600
www.jap4performance.com
Supplier of Marzocchi, Bitubo, EMC and Ohlins suspension parts.

NJB Shocks
Tel: 01206 330 631
www.njbshocks.co.uk
Classic black/chrome shock absorbers.

Suzuki

Crooks Suzuki, Barrow in Furness, Cumbria, England
Tel: 01229 822 120
www.crooks-suzuki.co.uk
Suzuki spares, advice, two-stroke specialist.

Straightline Racing, Suffolk, England
Tel: 01553 772 774
Air-cooled Suzuki fours specialist, tuning, spares, rebuilds.

Tools

Draper Tools
Tel: 023 8049 4333
www.draper.co.uk

Huge range of tools and workshop equipment. Trading since 1919.

Tracy Tools, Torquay, Devon, England
Tel: 01803 328 603
www.tracytools.com
Specialist tap and dies, drills, cutters, reamers, etc.

Uni-Thread
Tel: 01803 867 832
www.uni-thread.com
Helical inserts, taps and dies, drills, chucks, etc.

Trailers
Dave Cooper Trailers, Wrotham, Kent, England
Tel: 01732 820 082
www.davecooper.co.uk
Clip-on bike racks, trailers from single bike to sidecar transportation.

Transfers
Classic Transfers, Wotton-under-Edge, Gloucestershire, England
Tel: 01454 260 596
Transfers accurately reproduced, full catalogue available.

George Herbert
Tel: 01392 860 414
Transfers and stickers, unobtainable items reproduced.

Triumph
Greystone Enterprises, Whitstable, Kent
Tel: 01227 861 100
www.triumphtigerspares.co.uk
Tiger Cub spares.

Pete Hammond Motorcycles, Cirencester Gloucestershire, England
Tel: 01285 640 098
www.hammondmotorcycles.co.uk
Wide range of Triumph parts, 1958 onwards.

Hawkshaw Motorcycles, Merseyside, England
Tel: 0151 931 4488
www.hawkshawmotorcycles.com
Wide range of Triumph spares, 1950s onwards.

Tony Hayward, Connahs Quay, Flintshire, England
Tel: 01244 830 776
Spares and tuning parts for Triumph twins and triples.

Norman Hyde, Rugby, Warwickshire, England
Tel: 01926 497 375
www.normanhyde.co.uk
Meriden and Hinckley spares, tuning kits, etc.

Rockerbox, Wrecclesham, Surrey, England
Tel: 01252 722 973
Triumph bikes serviced and repaired, engines re-built.

Carl Rosner Ltd., South Croyden, Surrey, England
Tel: 020 8657 0121
www.carlrosner.co.uk
Spares and service for Triumph unit twins and triples, plus Hinckley models.

Shropshire Classic Motorcycles
Tel: 01743 860 146
www.triumphbonneville.com
Complete range of T140 Bonneville spares, brake disc upgrades, etc.

Tri-Supply, Honiton, Devon, England
Tel: 01404 47001
Email: triumph-meriden@trisupply.co.uk
Pre-Unit and unit Triumph twins specialist, Amal, Boyer, Renold, Toga parts supplied mail order.

Wilemans Motors, Derby, Derbyshire, England
Tel: 01332 342 813
Spares for 350-750cc Triumph twins, agents for Amal, Lucas, Boyer, Renold, etc.

L P Williams, Lancaster, Lancashire, England
Tel: 01524 770 956
www.triumph-spares.co.uk
Huge stocks of Triumph spares, repairs, tuning, etc. Established 1976.

Tyres

Vintage Tyres
Tel: 0845 1200 711
www.vintagetyres.com
Classic tyre specialist.

Vincent

Vin Parts, Llandindrod Wells, Wales
Tel: 01597 851 542
www.vintech.co.uk
Vincent and HRD spares, online ordering service.

Wheels

Central Wheel Components, Birmingham, England
Tel: 08444 706 816
www.central-wheel.co.uk
Chrome, alloy and stainless steel wheel rims, wheel building service and tyres.

Hagon Products Ltd, Hainault, Essex, England
Tel: 0208 502 6222
www.hagon-shocks.co.uk
Manufacturer of classic wheels, cast wheels repaired, wheelbuilding.

Yamaha

Granby Motors, Ilkeston, Derbyshire, England
Tel: 0115 944 1346
parts@granbymotors.net
General classic Japanese spares, Yamaha specialist.

Moto Link, New York, Lincolnshire, England
Tel: 01526 344 443
www.yamahaspares.uk.com
As new, old stock Yamaha parts.

PGM Yamaha
01289 386 720
www.pgmyamaha.com

Taymar Racing, Meopham, Kent, England
www.taymar-racing.co.uk
Yamaha two-stroke specialist, tuning, rebuilds.

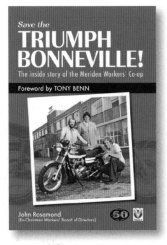

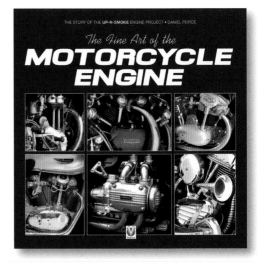

Written by the ex-Chairman of the famous Workers' Co-op, this is the real story of the last bastion of traditional British motorcycle production following the collapse of the industry. It's also the tale of a workforce's refusal to let the Triumph Bonneville die ...

£24.99
ISBN: 978-1-845842-65-9
Hardback • 448 pages
• 116 colour & b/w pictures

Gives a unique insight to the atmosphere and excitement of working in the AMC (Matchless/AJS) motorcycle factory. An inspiring story, supported by a host of period photographs and rare documents, providing a fascinating record of life within the British motorcycle industry from its heyday and on into decline and oblivion.

£17.99
ISBN: 978-1-84584-179-9
Hardback • 128 pages
c. 100 mainly b&w photos

Professional photographer Dan Peirce presents 64 stunning pictures from his popular 'Up-n-Smoke' engine project. The book also tells the story behind the project and how it took years to bring it from an inspired idea to a tangible reality. "Pornography for Gearheads"
– Cycle World magazine

£19.99
ISBN: 978-1-845841-74-4
Hardback • 144 pages
89 colour photos

For more info on Veloce titles, visit our website at www.veloce.co.uk
email info@veloce.co.uk • tel: +44 (0)1305 260068 • prices subject to change • p+p extra

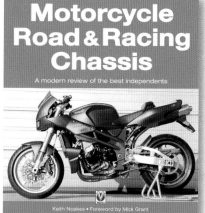

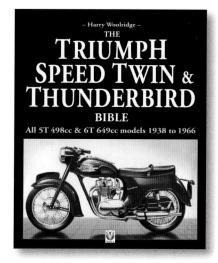

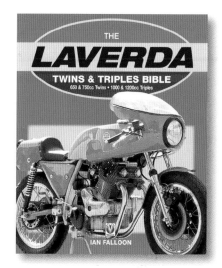

An account of the independent companies and individuals who have played a major part in the design and advancement of motorcycle frame (chassis) performance. With full specifications for many chassis and extensively illustrated throughout, this book is a must for any motorcycle enthusiast, and a valuable reference for the trade.

£19.99
ISBN: 978-1-845841-30-0
Paperback • 176 pages
246 mainly colour photos

The complete technical development history of the Triumph Speed Twin and Thunderbird motorcycles, and an invaluable reference source to identification, specification, exact year of manufacture and model type. A must for all Triumph lovers.

£25.00
ISBN: 978-1-904788-26-3
Hardback • 144 pages
142 colour & b&w photos

The large capacity Laverda twins and triples were some of the most charismatic and exciting motorcycles produced in a golden era. With a successful endurance racing programme publicizing them, Laverda's twins soon earned a reputation for durability. Here is the year-by-year, model-by-model, change-by-change record.

£29.99
ISBN: 978-1-845840-58-7
Hardback • 160 pages
150 mainly colour photos

For more info on Veloce titles, visit our website at www.veloce.co.uk
email info@veloce.co.uk • tel: +44 (0)1305 260068 • prices subject to change • p+p extra

Index

(Courtesy Graham Tansley)

(Courtesy John Chatterton)